To Bob

Many thanks,
Best Wishes Paul.

HAVE BOOTS WILL TRAVEL

HAVE BOOTS WILL TRAVEL

THE STORY OF FRANK LARGE

BY PF LARGE

First published by Pitch Publishing, 2014
Pitch Publishing
A2 Yeoman Gate
Yeoman Way
Durrington
BN13 3QZ
www.pitchpublishing.co.uk

A CIP catalogue record is available for this book from the British Library.

ISBN 978 1 90962 628 7

Typesetting and origination by Pitch Publishing
Printed in Great Britain

Contents

Acknowledgements

MANY thanks to all the team at Pitch Publishing for all the work they have done on this project and their patience as it unfolded.

To Frank Grande without whom this book would not have been possible!

The contributions of Alan Poole, Phil Rostron and Keiran Cooke are inspired and are greatly appreciated.

Thanks to all the players and managers I managed to get to talk to (sadly not all are still with us); their time and kind words were always a joy. A special thanks to Bob Worthington and his wife Julie for their great kindness.

Finally, a big thanks to my family for their support and encouragement.

To my wife Angie and my two daughters Stephanie and Hannah

Introduction

FOR 11 years, from the mid-1970s to the mid-1980s, Frank Large, who had retired from football, worked in a local chemical factory on shifts – six days a week including 12 hours on both Saturdays and Sundays, over 60 hours per week.

Like millions of other working men he did it to provide for his family, to clothe, house and feed us. He didn't grumble, he got on with it. It was hard, dirty, difficult and monotonous work and while the money was OK, the weekends were lost for a decade. Nobody thanked him. We took it for granted and he accepted his duty.

When he was diagnosed with cancer he accepted the news stoically, didn't complain and approached it like it was another shift to be completed.

On the day he died, I thanked him for being my dad and especially for those years he had done in the factory. I was never more proud of him doing that.

I promised myself that I would try and tell Frank's story as he deserved it. He was a man of few words, not prone to displaying emotions but loving, caring, honest and loyal nonetheless. Frank was proud of his family and its achievements and a bloody good footballer to boot.

When I discovered the wealth of goodwill that still existed within the game for him my task became a pleasure, full of wonderful stories and amazing characters.

My only regret is that Frank never got to hear it for himself. Mind you, knowing him, he would have taken it in his stride, enjoyed the laughs, the memories and the beers, but played it down without letting it go to his head.

That was Frank's way.

1

Sir Bobby Robson

WE had stored all of the photos, programmes and cuttings Mum had kept of Frank's career in an ancient battered grey suitcase. The suitcase (once visited regularly when we were growing up) eventually got put away in the attic, rarely seeing the light of day.

As Frank fought his terrible illness that long hot summer of 2003, I took the suitcase and over the space of a few days, pasted every snippet, photo and article into a massive wallpaper album. Completed, I took it in to the local hospital one weekend, where Frank was having more treatment.

I sat with him as he flicked through and had an amazing time as names were remembered, faces recognised and matches recalled. It dawned on me that these memories deserved to be properly recorded and I started kicking around the idea of writing a book. I even drew up a list of past players and managers to contact.

However by this time Frank was very weak and I knew it would probably be quite a strain for him, so I decided against it. Knowing that he had only a little time left, it felt ghoulish to even consider interviewing him. The idea was shelved and the list binned.

It took Sir Bobby Robson's involvement with the Football Association of Ireland to re-ignite the project and when I saw him on *RTE News* in Portmarnock with the Ireland national squad I decided to grab the bull by the horns – his name was on the top of the list and it felt like the right thing to do. Anyway I had nothing to lose.

So that April in 2007 I phoned the team hotel in the faint hope that I might get to talk to him, and was delighted that later that afternoon he took the time to get back to me.

The notion that I could begin researching a book on Frank had been re-ignited by the fact that Sir Bobby had chosen to mention about him in his own autobiography *Farewell But Not Goodbye* (Hodder and Stoughton, 2005). And now this footballing legend was polite enough to ring me back.

The actual conversation was extremely pleasant and when he asked after Frank I had to break the news that he had died (with hardly any comment in the national press) over four years earlier. Of course we touched ever so briefly on the cause and quickly moved on to the reason for me contacting him – 'the book'. We agreed that I should contact him again in the autumn and that I would be able to travel up and interview him regarding his and Frank's time at Fulham, and most importantly why he had included a paragraph on him in his own book.

Delighted with myself I didn't consider it again until I heard that summer that Sir Bobby's own cancer had returned and that the prognosis wasn't good. Selfishly I thought about my options and how this news affected my plans for a book on Frank. I wanted to interview him before it was too late and considered travelling to Newcastle, but would he be able or willing to see me?

However as perspective (as it had four years earlier) kicked in I resigned myself to the fact that the last thing he needed was a former player's son pestering him to talk about insignificant events that happened 39 years ago. I resigned myself to the fact that the opportunity had passed again and that I probably wouldn't get to write the book about Frank that I promised to do.

13 October 2007

To my surprise I read that despite his illness Sir Bobby has travelled over to Dublin to assist manager Steve Staunton as Ireland prepare to face Germany in a crucial 2008 European Championships qualifier.

I phoned the hotel and am shocked that the receptionist is going to put my call directly through to his room. I explained that I didn't want to disturb him and that I would prefer just to leave a message. Message left, 30 minutes later he phones me and agrees to see me the next day at 2pm. Having kindly given me his mobile number, I confirm the appointment by text, 90 per cent certain that Sir Bobby probably doesn't do text. I leave County Mayo on the wild Atlantic coast of Ireland at 10am the following day in the pouring rain with Sir Bobby's autobiography, Frank's scrapbook and a notepad with four very ordinary questions.

The reason for the interview was simple: Why did he include Frank, a player he reluctantly signed and only managed for less than three months, in his autobiography?

How can he still remember him 40 years later, after literally managing thousands of players in between?

The sun is shining as I drive into Portmarnock. Ireland had held Germany 0-0, an outstanding performance and an excellent result, but it is not enough and it is effectively the end of the campaign for 2008.

Having failed to get the hotel's address I pick the most obvious-looking candidate; a large, posh-looking hotel, sitting on a bluff overlooking the sea.

I park up and wander in to reception. With no Garda (police) or security I feel that I might have made a mistake and ask the receptionist if this is the right hotel. She nods and when I ask if Sir Bobby is here she goes to pick up the phone and is obviously about to call the room. I am 45 minutes early and feel very English when asking her not to bother him. I feel like saying that this is Sir Bobby Robson and you don't just be calling his room for any Tom, Dick, Harry or Paul.

Instead I thank her and go for a walk by the golf course. To settle my nerves and give me a chance to improve my four questions I go to the clubhouse and over a very disappointing pint of Guinness fail miserably to tickle up the offending questions. In fact as I look at them the four have merged into two, 'Why did you sign him?' and 'Why did you put him into your book?'

Seven hours-plus of driving across a whole country to ask a footballing legend two relatively inane questions. Too late the time has come and I arrive at reception early (a habit picked up off Frank, he was actually early for his own funeral!) and the same happy receptionist points out to me that Sir Bobby is in the foyer. I spot him 20 yards away and wander over with the scrapbook, notepad and his book.

Sir Bobby is surprised when he looks up from the sports pages of his Sunday newspaper and sees his own face staring back at him from the cover of his book. 'Oh you've got my book,' he states.

I know he hasn't a clue who I am, so I introduce myself and go to sit down. Still puzzled, he looks at me and I realise that he has forgotten I was coming. I quickly remind him about the arrangement and he slowly begins to understand the situation. Charley Woods (formerly of Newcastle United and Crystal Palace) offers me his chair and I sit down alongside Sir Bobby.

I offer him my hand and thank him for his time. He looks very frail but his white hair is immaculately cut and brushed, his skin a little pale but his blue eyes look alert and healthy. He carries his left arm across his chest and it looks like he only has partial use of it.

I notice his white trainers with Velcro fasteners, and remember that Frank wore the same towards the end – easy to get on and off. He spots the A4-sized photo of Frank on the cover of his playing record and asks to see it. He carefully holds it up and says, 'Ahh yes that's him!'

I immediately get a lump in my throat. 'When did he die?' he asks. I answer and probably go into too much detail about his cancer. Sir Bobby just nods and I move on.

'So you are writing a book on your dad then,' he says. I answer that I am in the process of researching and that I am very honoured that he was prepared to give up some of his time.

'We've met before,' I tell him. He looks puzzled again and I quickly add that it was 39 years ago and that I was the freckly, red-haired, six-year-old at the dinner that followed Frank's signing for Fulham in the summer of 1968. Not a glimmer of recognition – not that I expected any.

He smiles patiently and I give him my first question, 'Why did you sign him?' He ponders the question and asks to be reminded of the month and year, and of course I immediately realise that while I know Frank's career inside out, Sir Bobby has probably only considered it twice in the past 39 years.

I start reading from his book, but he interrupts me and asks to be handed the copy. He carefully puts on his glasses and begins to read the three or four pages that deal not just with Frank but also his short stint as Fulham manager.

He closes the book and I feel that there is a clear recognition of the facts and Sir Bobby begins to explain how Matt Gillies (the Leicester City manager) phoned him with his offer (cash and Frank for Allan Clarke) and how he and Harry Haslam (chief scout) felt along with the club secretary and chairman that it was the best deal for Fulham.

'Did Frank have any say over the deal?' I ask and his reaction is instant, a wry smile and a little laugh. 'There were no agents in them days – players were bought and sold like cattle,' Sir Bobby replies.

'Did Allan Clarke insist on leaving?' Sir Bobby fixes me with an intense stare, 'He did, we wanted to keep him, you don't want to lose any of your good young players but...'

At that moment three young boys arrive and ask me if I am a famous footballer. I smile and tell them that I am not but that this man is. With impeccable manners they ask for his autograph and pen and paper are readied. Sir Bobby, with some difficulty, writes their names and signs his own. No sooner had they left than the youngest scampers back – coaxed by his dad – and asks, 'Can you get me a jersey?' Without looking up Sir Bobby says politely but firmly, 'Sorry son, not possible.'

Back to 1968 and I ask, 'What made you turn down more money from Manchester United?' Sir Bobby strokes his nose and for the first time I see him get animated – this is a real memory. 'Your dad was valued at around £30,000. I knew we had to replace Allan and knew that at the time you couldn't get much for that kind of money. The club needed the cash and I needed a centre-forward, it was the best deal for Fulham.'

Sir Bobby is flowing and I try to keep it going. 'Had you seen Frank? What qualities did he have that attracted you?'

'Oh yes,' he smiles. 'He was a great team player; honest, hard-working and very good in the air.' Sir Bobby is looking past me, over my shoulder and towards the reception desk, this is what he does best and the flow is fast and efficient. 'He wasn't the best technically, he wasn't like…' He falters as he searches for an example but continues regardless. 'He was more like an old-fashioned centre-forward, a battering ram. Yes, yes he reminded me of Bedford Jezzard, I played with him at Fulham you know. Yes Frank was like that, excellent in the air and very very brave.'

'I have heard it said,' I venture, 'that with Johnny Haynes in the team a direct approach was not going to happen and that as a result Frank struggled.'

I asked the question not having thought of it before in the hope that it might help explain Frank's complete loss of form and consequent struggle that befell him at Fulham. Sir Bobby contemplates it and begins to answer with his good hand drawing imaginary patterns in the air.

'Yes, Johnny could pass the ball, probably the best passer of the ball in England, the idea was that he would get the ball to the wingers…' Another pause as he struggles to remember the wide men's names, and I attempt to help by delving into the records, but realise we'll lose the flow so nudge him with 'and they would put into the box for Frank'. 'Yes that was it, he was brave you know, a real handful, and a great, great header.'

Frank is quoted as saying that the only player he was ever afraid of on the football pitch was Johnny Haynes. Why would he say that ? Was he a bully?'

Sir Bobby thinks about this and I can see that he picks his words very carefully. 'Johnny was a perfectionist; he often couldn't understand why other players weren't as good. I said to him, "Johnny you have to realise that you're Johnny Haynes"!' If there is even the slightest hint of criticism he quickly follows up with, 'Johnny was a great player and a great lad.' I begin to understand how this man has survived in the game with his reputation intact for over 60 years.

I ask him if he ever went back to Craven Cottage (he wrote that at the time of his sacking he made a vow never to return). 'Aye lad, I do, it was a long time ago…a lot of water under the bridge, but it hurt, hurt like hell, it was my first job.' Sir Bobby is obviously a little upset and a little flustered so I try and move on.

When I had first made contact with him in the spring I asked if it was OK to send correspondence via Newcastle United. Realising what I had said, I said that maybe that wasn't a good thing since he had fallen out with them. Quick as a flash he said, 'No son, they fell out with me!' They had sacked him unceremoniously in August 2004.

At this moment a young lad, badly crippled from the waist down, hobbles on crutches towards the hotel door. Sir Bobby points and says, 'That puts life into perspective.' 'Hey Charlie,' he adds, as Charlie looks up from his Sunday paper a few yards away. 'See that Charlie, that puts life into perspective.'

Charlie wanders over and Sir Bobby says, 'Hey Charlie, Paul's writing a book on his father Frank. Charlie used to play for Newcastle and Crystal Palace.' I ask if he played against Frank. 'Ee man I did,' replies Charlie, another Geordie. 'He was a hard man, difficult to mark and he could score,' he adds while smiling, before joining us at our table.

I realise that the interview is coming to an end; a messenger arrives to inform Sir Bobby that there is a team meeting in 15 minutes. Sir Bobby is picking over the scrapbook, immensely impressed as is Charlie, both seeing faces and teams from their youth. I ask Sir Bobby my main question: 'Why did you mention him in your book? You managed thousands of players, why Frank?'

A smile spreads across his face but no answer. Charlie asks a question and the moment is lost. Albert Quixall and Theo Foley are discussed and I change tack. 'When you signed Frank we went for a meal,' and he nods in recognition. 'When my younger brother poured salt on his meal the lid came off and emptied the contents over his plate.' Laughter follows. 'You did that didn't you?' No answer but he continues to laugh, wrinkling his nose, his eyes alive.

By now I have been there for nearly an hour and Sir Bobby is getting ready for the team meeting. I ask him to sign my copy of his book and he writes:

> 'Best Wishes Paul
> Enjoy my book – but –
> Enjoy even more, writing
> About your Dad !
> He's in here – but you
> Can write lots more!
> Bobby Robson'

Delighted, I thank him and Charlie for their time. As I'm getting ready to go I ask again why he mentioned Frank in his book and at last comes a reply, 'He was a decent lad.' We shake hands and say goodbye.

Walking back to the car I feel absolutely brilliant as the former England, Barcelona and Newcastle manager and recognised full-time football legend has confirmed something I had known for as long as I could remember.

Later that year Sir Bobby was presented with a lifetime achievement award at the BBC Sports Personality of the Year ceremony. Watching avidly as he got up to an emotional standing ovation and very carefully picked his way to the stage, I started to cry. Surprised (I don't do crying, I had got that from Frank, I had never seen him cry once!), it became more intense, and I started sobbing uncontrollably, chest heaving dramatically, and was relieved there was nobody else in the room to see my embarrassment.

Presentation over, as Sir Bobby got back to his seat I finally managed to control myself and I realised immediately that I was not just overcome with the spontaneous out-pouring of love and emotion the great man inspired but that I was crying the tears I had held back when Frank had died four years earlier.

'I also made a huge profit on Allan Clarke when we sold him to Leicester for £120,000 cash plus Frank Large in part-exchange. What a great lad Frank was – not technically gifted but strong and powerful. He could bundle his way through any traffic jam of bodies.' Sir Bobby Robson, 2005.

2

Leeds

FRANK was born on 26 January 1940, the first-born of Richard and Hilda (Leuty), in the Danubes off Geldered Road, Holbeck, Leeds.

Appropriately Geldered Road led at one end to the Cattle Market, and more significantly at the other, towards the home of Leeds United less than a mile from Frank's birthplace.

Home was a simple back-to-back red-brick terrace. Eight houses formed a block, and the blocks were separated by a yard that had the shared toilets. Common to the north of England these houses provided a cheap and simple solution to accommodating a lot of people in a relatively small area, ideal for housing the labourers of the Industrial Revolution that flocked into the burgeoning towns and cities of the Midlands and the North.

Officially banned in 1909, Leeds somehow managed to keep constructing them into the 1930s, the basic lay-out being two small rooms downstairs and two above, often with a room in the attic.

Holbeck was an industrial enclave, south-west of the city centre, criss-crossed by the railways that were driven into the city in the early 1800s. Iron foundries, flax and woollen mills (including the famous Temple Works), railway engineering works and numerous other factories competed for space in a densely populated area. By the time of the Second World War it was already in decline.

Richard (known as Dick) was descended from Welsh stock and like many, moved north looking for work. Hilda's roots were slightly more exotic as the Leutys were French Huguenots (Protestants) who fled to England in the early 1800s as a result of religious persecution.

Dick had survived a bad fall when constructing one of the many cooling towers that surrounded the city. He had broken his back, but fortunately not his spine, and as a result he wore a thick leather belt around his waist for the rest of his days. He worked in a local chemical works and Hilda was a seamstress. He was 40 when Frank was born, 18 years older than Hilda, and they went on to have two more sons, Stan and John.

Despite being a major industrial city with a significant railway hub and munitions factories (AVRO produced Lancaster Bombers from its plant at RAF Yeadon, now Leeds/Bradford Airport), Leeds got off lightly during the war, as the Luftwaffe only undertook nine raids.

The largest on 14 and 15 March 1941 did however result in substantial damage, with the city centre, Holbeck, Beeston, Armley and Bramley bearing the brunt. Sixty-five people were killed and along with the Town Hall and the New Station being hit, 100 houses were destroyed and 4,600 were damaged. Fortunately the Danubes survived intact.

Frank attended the local school, Ingram Road, and while he didn't excel academically he was a voracious reader and had an amazing ability for spelling. As a kid doing my homework I often remember being staggered that Frank could spell the most ridiculous words.

Football was a big part of his early life and visits to Elland Road were recalled in later years with Tom Finney selected as his own personal hero. Games on street corners with home-made balls were the norm. He represented the school but failed to gain selection for any of the Leeds Boys teams.

In the early 1950s Hilda was diagnosed with tuberculosis and sent to a sanatorium on the outskirts of the city. TB was an endemic disease of the urban poor and prior to the discovery of antibiotics was a killer, possibly being responsible for 25 per cent of all deaths.

The sanitoria for the poor often resembled prisons with a regime of fresh air and labour and with Hilda away Frank moved to his grandma Sally's house, in Armley, just below the jail. Looked after by his aunty Amelia (Meelie), Hilda's younger sister, he was never happier, and a strong bond grew between them.

Frank's childhood wasn't easy. While he was loved his parents didn't show much affection and the house wasn't comfortable or homely. Both his Mum and Dad were heavy smokers and when Frank was 12 his Dad caught him smoking. Dick sat him down and made him smoke enough cigarettes until he was sick! Frank never smoked again.

I remember staying with them as a child in their council house in Belle Isle and being woken up by the pair of them coughing their guts up.

The house was sparsely furnished. A tin pail was utilised as a fridge while there were no light shades and no carpets.

They never once went to see him play a professional game even though they were very proud of him, a fact that upset Frank, yet Dick would write a lovely letter every week to Frank telling him all the news and sending love.

Upon leaving school he got a job with British Rail as an apprentice fire man, responsible for setting the fire in the fire box and keeping it going on the steam engines that still dominated the rail network. It was hard work but he loved it, and he kept his passion for steam all his life. Any book on steam trains made a perfect Christmas or birthday present. One of the lines running out of Leeds was to Carlisle (the old LNER) and he once got to drive the engine as it steamed over the world-famous Ribblehead Viaduct, west of Settle.

Frank's pals were local lads Jack Stancliffe and Hughy King who both spent a little time at Her Majesty's Pleasure over an incident in the Hanover pub. Luckily Frank wasn't there that night (he was away on duty with Halifax) or he could well have been in trouble as well.

It was meeting my Mum that settled him down. Frank was out with his mates in the Mecca dance hall, resplendent in his Halifax Town blazer and slacks, when he was spotted by Aileen. It was love at first sight. Within a year they were engaged and they got married in August 1961, and Frank was allowed one day off before returning to pre-season training.

The advantage of being married was that he became eligible for a club house and they moved to Halifax as soon as possible.

Mum came from an Irish Catholic family and had six brothers and five sisters. Home was a Victorian manse, formerly a vicarage, 8 Hall Lane. This amazing house was a hive of activity with people always coming and going, and Frank settled in and like many others became an extended member of the family.

Food was always being cooked, served or eaten and as a youngster I loved the place with its massive cellar (used by my uncles as a garage), a servants' back-stair that led off the kitchen and a large stained glass window that looked across the city towards Headingley. Hide and seek with my cousins in that house was deadly.

As a child we regularly got into the car on a Sunday and drove to Leeds, wherever we were in the country. The ritual would be the same. Frank would make the decision and we as kids agreed instantly, while Mum was left to gather up babies and pack changing bags. We meanwhile would be sat in the car, engine running, and Frank – impatient as ever – would often beep the horn to let her know we were ready to go. Mum did not take kindly to this at all.

With the drive to Leeds over, we would approach Armley on the new ring road and Frank would theatrically point to a spot on the road and say, 'That's where my house was!' The Danubes had been demolished in the late 1960s as Leeds strove to remove the blight of the back-to-backs they had only just stopped building. Whole swathes of the city were levelled and it looked like the Luftwaffe had been back to carpet-bomb the place.

Leeds positioned itself as the 'Motorway City of the 70s' and as the inner ring road brought havoc to the neighbourhoods unfortunate enough to be in its way, Poulson and his cronies made big bucks by building 'brutalist' monstrosities such as the International Pool and the City House, as they looked to make Leeds the 'Capital of the North'.

Pulling up at Grandma's, Frank would be out of the car, round up a couple of willing brothers-in-law and be off to the local for a few jars. Upon their return dinner was served, always Yorkshire pudding and gravy first as a starter, followed by roast beef and the veg. Often there would be a dozen or more folk sitting down, and plenty more coming and going.

We then called out to Granddad Dick's and had a light supper before heading home for a quick bath and to be ready for school the next day. Heaven.

Frank was always proud of his Yorkshire roots. He never lost his accent and would happily sing a verse of 'Ilkley Moor' if required (or he was drunk enough), but it was Leeds he was most proud of. Along with the football team he loved the place and always felt at home there.

That is strange when you think he left at the age of 21 never to live there again, or maybe it is not so strange when everything is considered.

3

Halifax Town

IDLY Googling Frank's name one quiet morning at work, a site called *Backpass* catches my eye, a retro football magazine 'for fans of football in the 1960s, 70s and 80s'. A picture of its first edition is shown and I instantly spot Frank smiling in the bottom-left corner. The photo is of him kneeling above a ball at Fulham in 1968, and is the one we placed on his coffin in Holy Trinity Church, Westport, in August 2003.

Unable to order a copy I manage to get a telephone number and get through to the editor, who very kindly sends me copies of the first two issues. The article in the first edition is the one by Alan Poole (see the chapter on Kettering Town) concerning Frank's short time with Ron Atkinson. The second edition contains a number of nice letters and remembrances from folk, one notably from Phil Rostron (see the chapter on Oldham).

Having decided to write Frank's story I write to Mike Berry, the editor, asking if he would put in a small piece about the book in the magazine asking for help from any ex-players, managers or fans who might have a good story about Frank.

With the article duly published in the next issue, I sit back and wait for the phone to ring convinced that all my research would be done for me, as numerous pros and fans alike from all his clubs would bombard me with sparkling anecdotes.

Some weeks later, having nearly forgotten about the article, I get a message at home to contact Bob Worthington who knows some of Frank's Halifax colleagues.

Delighted, I phone Bob and quickly realise that the softly-spoken man is one of the three famous footballing brothers from Halifax. Dave had played with Halifax and the other brother was Frank, the much travelled maverick, who I would regularly see in Leeds nightclubs in the early 80s (Thursday nights, breaking club rules!).

Bob very kindly offers to organise a meeting with a scattering of lads who played with Frank, including Alex South and Eric Harrison. The meeting is settled for August 2009 in Yorkshire. I thank Bob and am amazed at his generosity.

Thursday 4 August

Stuck in traffic on the ring road in Bradford and close to losing the will to live, I notice that the sign for the A63 is marked Halifax and realise that 47 years ago, to the day, I was possibly leaving the hospital in Halifax as an infant ready to follow Frank on his peripatetic journey around England. To my knowledge I had never been back, though I was always proud of the fact that I was a native, and along with John Noakes and the Building Society I keenly followed the Shaymen.

As I approach the town, the sun is shining and the traffic flowing. I cross the Calder river and try and take in as much of the place as I can.

Neat and tidy with some old mills and chimneys wedged into a steep valley is all I can observe as I climb out of the other side of the valley. No signs for The Shay or a clue as to the whereabouts of the house that Mum and Dad lived in, a house I possibly never even went to (I was born at the end of July 1962, and Frank had already signed for QPR and was in 'digs' in London, and Mum was staying at her parents' in Leeds).

Bob Worthington is 63 years young; tall, athletically built, trim, a full head of hair, greying slightly at the temple. After he opens the door, and with introductions done, I tell him there's no way he played against Frank for Notts County in 1970 as he looks younger than me! Laughing he assures me he did and introduces his lovely wife Julie who looks like a young Helen Mirren.

I give Bob this quarter's edition of *Backpass*, which coincidently has a young Frank Worthington on the cover. I ask if Frank is coming to the meeting and I'm disappointed that he can't make it, but chuffed to be told that as a boy Frank Worthington worshipped Frank Large.

Brother Dave (a top scout on the continent for Blackburn Rovers) arrives tanned and fit-looking so we head of to the pub to meet the rest of the lads.

The bar is situated right next to the Rochdale canal and as we pull up Dave waves to two fellas sitting out in the evening sunshine. With the scrapbook under my arm I walk over and am introduced to Alex South and Eric Harrison.

As I shake Alex's hand his eyes light up and with a distinctly southern accent (he had lived up north for the best part of 60 years!) he floors me with, 'Fucking hell Largey's lad, you look just like him. You know your Dad was my fucking hero!'

Before I get to ask him why, with beers ordered and drinkers seated, Alex starts on a story about when Frank first went to Halifax – Alex's memory is almost photographic and all night long he is the one to put a name, a date or a venue on any memory, not bad for a man of 79 years with a military bearing and a friendly face.

'Your Dad turned up for training one day, the manager Harry Hooper said nothing, he didn't even introduce him, just put him into the practice match. Two hours later he'd kicked every one of us, but we took an instant shine to him, his energy and enthusiasm had impressed us all.'

More beers are produced and despite my efforts to get them in, it appears that not only are they going to treat me to loads of stories but also a good piss-up. Eric is nodding as Alex continues, 'He was scruffy he had holes in his jeans, not like my grandchildren's designer holes, they were torn and worn out, and his shoes had holes in the bottom and his hair was long and lank and his face was pockmarked, he looked like an urchin!

'After the training session the manager gave him his blazer, I gave him my shoes and some of the other lads gave him shirts and trousers, and he left the best-dressed man in Halifax.'

I am still laughing when Eric asks if he came from a rough part of Leeds. This is Eric Harrison the world-famous youth coach at Manchester United (brought to Manchester by Ron Atkinson, who phoned to tell him of Frank's death) who nurtured a whole generation of stars like David Beckham, Ryan Giggs and Paul Scholes, and all those years ago Frank's best mate at Halifax. I reply that he did.

'I thought as much,' came the reply. 'One day he arrived for training [he used to get the bus from Leeds] and he wasn't himself – not very happy at all. Eventually I got it out of him – he was in a bit of bother with a local gang and he was worried, not like your Dad. I asked if he needed any help and was shocked when he asked if we'd come over to Leeds to help him sort it out.'

Dave picks up the story, 'I was just 17 years old and on the books. Your Dad asked us all, three or four apprentices, me and Eric to come over the next night. We quietly agreed and your Dad set off for the bus. Seconds later he turned and said, "Oh aye and make sure you bring some tools, bike chains, hammers, you'll need 'em".'

Eric smiles, 'We were bricking it, the next day when Frank turned up for training – excuses were ready! He didn't mention a word, until after the session, when he quietly said that we weren't needed and that it was sorted – by god were we happy.'

Alex has produced a set of old Halifax programmes that the lads are signing. He pushes one towards me and tells me that the owner wants me to sign it. I tell Alex that it's many years since I signed my Dad's name (I got caught signing a dodgy school report in the mid-1970s).

'No, you've to sign your own name,' is the instruction and an ancient programme from April 1961 vs QPR is presented. This is surreal. Here I am signing my own name on a programme published before I was born. I quickly scribble my name and am passed another, when I realise that the other lads had taken a great deal more effort and pride when signing and that mine (I sign a great deal of papers every day at work and have managed after 20 years, to get my name down to two scruffy squiggles) is an embarrassment.

I feel a little guilty and that I've somehow managed to let myself and, by proxy, Frank down. I sign the rest of the programmes in a style I had not used since being a teenager, when I used to practise signing my name on any spare scrap of paper.

More drinks are brought and despite my protestations, I am not allowed to put my hand in my pocket. I ask Eric about the time that Don Revie tapped up Frank (an illegal approach to a contracted player). 'Yes it did happen, your Dad begged me to go and ask Harry [the manager of Halifax] for a transfer to Leeds. He wouldn't come in and sat outside Harry's office. I went in and told him that Leeds [then in the Second Division] wanted me and your Dad. Harry just shook his head and said, "No way!" That was that. I went back outside and told your Dad, who was pacing up and down the corridor. He was absolutely crestfallen, he kept repeating, "My home-town club, I always wanted to play for them." That was the way it was in them days, the clubs and managers had all the power.'

Eric doesn't mention that, allegedly, Revie had approached Frank in a bar in Leeds and attempted to get him to leave Halifax. Frank told me that a combination of Leeds wanting him on the cheap – as he was a local lad – and

Halifax's reluctance to sell to local rivals scuppered the deal. He always regretted the fact that he never got the chance to play for his beloved Leeds.

I ask Eric if he thinks a player of Frank's calibre could play today. 'Oh god yes, but not as a centre-forward, those days of a battering-ram centre-forward are gone, there would be no place today for that, but I say he could quite easily have been a Vieira type-player.'

Great praise from a shrewd judge. 'Your Dad had a great engine, he could get penalty box to penalty box, was brilliant in the air, and could pass and also tackle – oh yes, he would have been good enough today.'

Delighted, I ask about the old-fashioned positions of left-half, wing-half and inside-forward. Alex gives a full explanation, which I nearly grasp, the key factor being for Frank was that he was running at the back three (his development into a centre-forward saw him playing with his back to the goal and took time!). With his strength and power he scored a lot of goals from what today we would call midfield – 52 goals in 141 appearances.

Alex is in great form and entertaining us all. He recalls a home game against Torquay (22 August 1960). 'I was recovering from an injury and was in the dug-out and remember that at the time there was no love lost between us and Torquay. It was a summer match and a heavy shower had made the surface perfect for a game, slick and lush. Towards the end of the game your Dad slid into a tackle with a Torquay player, who had been kicking him all night long. He foolishly started wrestling with Frank as they slid impressively towards the dug-out. Your Dad reacted instinctively, catching this poor fellow's head under his arm, and I'll never forget, he punched him furiously like a boxer – short quick jabs, I reckon he knocked him out.' All the lads are laughing at the memory that saw Frank sent off for the first time.

As the night winds down I manage to catch Alex before he leaves and ask him why Frank, who was ten years younger, was his hero. 'Your Dad was one of the very few players who I played with, or against, who could change a game on his own. He never gave up and regularly made something happen out of nothing. The only other player I played with like that was Willie Carlin, Frank's best mate when they both played for Carlisle in that memorable season 1964/65.'

Before he goes Alex tells me he saw Frank score the best headed goal he had seen in all his life. 'He climbed and twisted, forcing a deflection into the goal with such power, simply unbelievable!'

It was a truly brilliant night, to meet with lads who knew Frank when he was a teenager and to enjoy a few beers, and to listen to their tales of the old days. I felt truly privileged and only wish that Frank would have got the chance, had he lived, to meet up with them again, those who were there when he set out on his footballing journey and followed his subsequent career with interest.

◆ ◆ ◆ ◆ ◆

In 1958 Frank was working for British Rail as an engine cleaner and got asked to play for the works team in the local half-holiday league (matches were played on a Wednesday afternoon to accommodate the many workers who couldn't play on Saturdays). Having played at school but not earned any representative honours, this relatively low level of football appeared to suit Frank (in the early 1980s while at university in Leeds I helped out our fifth team, once, in this league, away to the Fforde Green pub, and I can testify to the poor quality of play and the reception we got as students! We had to run to the minibus in fear of our lives!).

However, fortunately for Frank a scout from Halifax spotted him and in January 1958, just before his 18th birthday, he signed amateur forms with the club, making his debut away to Harrogate Railway, in the West Riding League Division Two. I have a picture of that team riding high in the division, Frank is on one knee at the front, looking impossibly young and ultra-skinny – a mere boy in his Stanley Matthews shorts and rugby-type jersey.

The rest of the team appear to be either over 35 years old or teenagers, and the trainer G. Fairburn is wearing a sheepskin jacket, flat cap and has his trousers tucked into his socks! That's now called a 'Waveller' look and is *de rigueur* in Ballina.

The training and coaching improved the raw talent and he turned professional in April 1959.

He made his debut for Halifax, at the Racecourse Ground, Wrexham, on 22 April in a 1-0 defeat and played the last three games of that season as Halifax finished a respectable ninth in the newly formed Third Division.

With Frank now a regular in Harry Hooper's team, Halifax got off to a flying start in 1959/60, a 1-0 defeat away to Colchester United their only reverse in their opening 13 matches. Playing at wing-half Frank opened his professional goalscoring account with two goals in a 3-2 victory over Colchester on 14 September in front of 6,254 fans.

Even with the welcome return of Alex South (back from an injury that kept him out for six months), as Christmas approached Halifax's form slumped and despite a good 4-0 win over local rivals Bradford City (the local paper reports under the headline 'Large stops City's run', 'Six goals in three matches from 19-year-old Frank Large, the Halifax inside-left, have given needed scoring power to the Town attack and the couple against Bradford City were sufficient to provide the Shaymen's first away victory since September 19th') and a winning competition debut for Frank in the FA Cup, the side struggled and failed to win any of their next nine league games.

On Boxing Day Frank was moved into the forwards and scored the goal that secured a home draw with Port Vale. Finally on 2 January as the 1960s dawned and with George Fagan back, after nine months out, Halifax won and Frank scored another in a 4-2 defeat of Mansfield.

A hat-trick against Barnsley (the first of his career; he scored three more, all for Northampton Town) in a 5-0 demolition was quickly followed by a brace away to Bradford City. Regardless of the odd outstanding victory (notably a 5-0 thrashing of Accrington Stanley) too many games were drawn or lost by the odd goal and Halifax settled at 15th, which was disappointing after the splendid start. Frank returned 17 goals in 46 appearances, not bad for his first full season.

Alex South spoke highly of Halifax and how they looked after the players and did things properly. A pre-season tour to Belgium and Holland that summer highlighted this. Frank sent a postcard to Mum from Brussels, telling her that several players fell asleep in a park until 2am, not revealing whether he was one of them! He did however confirm that he would get the 'cloggs' for Dolly.

The Halifax Town players' ticket for the 1960/61 season makes interesting reading, notably the Players' Instructions 5:

> 'Smoking is strictly forbidden on match-days and before training – dancing after Wednesday night is strictly forbidden – motor-cycling is also strictly forbidden.'

Surprisingly no mention of drink (Frank told me that the club used to provide him with a crate of Guinness a week, in the hope that it would build him up!), pubs or nightclubs. I am sure Alex, Eric, Dave and the lads, as good pros, didn't need any direction regarding booze.

It was the second match of that campaign, at home to Torquay, that Alex recalled so vividly. Back from suspension and back to wing-half, it took seven games for him to register his first goal of the season and he then struck five in his next five outings.

In a reasonable league position at Christmas, the 6-2 humiliation of Southend on 24 December was special to Frank. He scored two and the local paper reported that 'when Frank Large hammered home his second goal after 51 minutes, he fulfilled a pre-match promise to score twice to celebrate his engagement today to a Leeds girl'.

They got married on 7 August 1961 and with the season less than a fortnight away, Frank got one day off. They had their honeymoon eight years later, in Spain, with me, Richard and David in tow.

As the New Year progressed Halifax's form dipped spectacularly, losing seven, drawing nine and winning only three of their games. The last game of the season. a 2-1 away win at Bournemouth (Frank scored both), was only their second away victory all year. All in all finishing ninth wasn't too bad.

Frank's performances were beginning to get him noticed outside of West Yorkshire.

Maurice Weedon, writing in the *Soccer Star* on 11 March 1961, charted Frank's career to date and noted his desire to progress. 'Large told me that his greatest ambition is to play for a First Division side and it is more than likely that he will do so before too long, for he has been the object of several enquiries and although Halifax do not wish to sell, he may move for two reasons. Attendances have been falling and the five-figure fee his move would bring would be most acceptable. The other reason is that Mr Hooper senior knows what a fine prospect Large is, and does not want to stand in his way of entering senior soccer.'

A string of top clubs appeared to be lining up to sign him and after the disappointment of being refused a move to Leeds, it seemed only a matter of time before he left The Shay.

Charlie Mitten, a 'desperate Newcastle manager ready to bid big money', was reported to be on a 'hush hush recruiting mission', with Frank the target. He was spotted at The Shay on 30 September 1961 to see Frank play against Northampton. A disappointing 3-1 defeat didn't do him any favours.

'Johnny Carey, the Goodison Park chief, is so keen on this all-action six-footer that he has asked Halifax specially to play him at left-half in the first team so that he can make a personal check on him,' read one report. The article doesn't mention Hooper's opinion on this matter, but it does go on to state that Frank had been the 'top player on Norwich's wanted list all season, but until now Halifax had been refusing all offers'.

The fact that the players had no say in this horse-trading was accepted, there were no agents and the slavery of the binding contracts and the maximum wage had only just been abolished.

By October Blackpool, then a mid-table outfit in the First Division, were interested and three directors travelled to The Shay to watch Frank and discuss a possible player exchange. Again it appeared that Mr Hooper was the potential stumbling block, according to the press, 'Mr Hooper stated today that Large could not leave The Shay unless the Town had the assurance of finding somebody strong enough in replacement.' The player being proposed was the Blackpool inside-forward Bruce Crawford.

Halifax struggled that season, finishing a lowly 18th with Frank managing 15 goals in 48 appearances. He scored his last goal for them in a 4-3 defeat at Ashton Gate against Bristol City and played his last match for them on 3 May 1962 – against, ironically, Queens Park Rangers.

Frank Large's Halifax Town record

	League		*FA Cup*		*League Cup*	
	Apps	*Gls*	*Apps*	*Gls*	*Apps*	*Gls*
1958/59	4	0	0	0	0	0
1959/60	44	17	2	0	0	0
1960/61	40	18	3	2	0	0
1961/62	46	15	1	0	1	0

Total (all competitions): 141 appearances, 52 goals

4

Queens Park Rangers

DESPITE all the interest from the big clubs it was Alec Stock who took Frank from The Shay to London and Queens Park Rangers for £7,500. Frank also secured a significant pay rise from £17 per week to £25. Despite the disappointment that he hadn't moved up a division or two (QPR just failed to gain promotion the previous season), he was joining a team hotly tipped to do well.

Frank joined a talented group of players, combining the experience of Roy Bentley and Tony Ingham with the wing wizardry of John McClelland and Mark Lazarus, the goal-grabbing forward Brian Bedford and local protege John Collins.

Interviewed in the opening day's match programme Frank was asked whether he had any thoughts on leaving his native Yorkshire. 'None at all, I always fancied playing for a London club, for one thing the weather is better down here!'

The interviewer wryly noted that they must have had some diabolical summers in Halifax lately. The article continued by saying that 'versatility ought to be his middle name, he has played wing-half, inside-forward and centre forward – which does he prefer?' Frank replied, 'Wing-half, but I'd play anywhere in a good side like Rangers.'

The article continued, 'The second big event for Frank this summer, in addition to his transfer, was the birth of a son, Paul, to his wife Aileen three weeks ago. In about a month's time Large will bring his wife and baby son from Halifax. They are to live in South Harrow. In saying welcome to Frank and wishing him every success in Rangers colours, we also say an advance "Welcome to London" to his family.' A nice touch.

The opening game of the 1962/63 season was at Loftus Road against Brighton, a 2-2 draw that saw Frank partnering Bedford up front. Two days later he moved back to left-half as former club Halifax arrived in London. QPR were defending a 100 per cent home record against the Shaymen, winning all of the previous three encounters (the old Third Divisions North and South were disbanded after the 1957/58 season, and both sides joined the new national Third Division in 1958). Bedford had scored seven goals in the last two meetings alone, and he scored two more in a 5-0 demolition. Four days later five more were scored at Brunton Park as Carlisle United were brushed aside 5-2.

The next match, away to Halifax, saw another comprehensive victory, 4-1 this time, putting QPR top of the table with 16 goals in just four games. As yet Frank had failed to score, but he was making a telling contribution from left-half. At The Shay his shrewd pass 'put Collins through and the Halifax captain Eric Harrison had no option but to pull him back. Angell coolly slotted home the subsequent penalty', according to one report. The second goal, after 20 minutes, saw 'Large smartly head back a Collins cross to Bedford, who scored after Downsborough had made a futile challenge'.

A 2-2 draw with Swindon saw Frank back up front and scoring his first goal for the Hoops. Having gone 1-0 down after 11 minutes, and struggling to break down the massed Swindon defence, a period of intense pressure saw the Robins' woodwork hit five times, before McClelland equalised. Two minutes later, following a mix-up in the Swindon defence, Frank swooped and headed home.

Unbelievably Rangers hit the woodwork again and were just about to go in at half-time with a deserved lead when on Swindon's second attack of the half Smith equalised. Apparently the second half failed to live up to the fireworks of the first.

Next up were local rivals Crystal Palace and in front of 16,853, 'Large stars in Rangers win...the 22-year-old appeared for the second time as the leader of the Rangers forward line and his thrustful, chase everything policy was a constant worry to the Palace backs. With the wingers Lazarus and McClelland he piled the pressure on a creaking Palace defence for most of the game.

'Large's tireless efforts brought him a peach of a goal which left 16,000 astounded and the whole Palace team stunned. The fantastic goal came from Frank Large in the closing minutes of the first half. Large received the ball from the right wing, he high kicked, hooking the ball over his shoulder into the back of the net.'

I presume that the term 'bicycle kick' was yet to be coined as the local reporter gamely struggles to describe Frank's effort.

Despite pulling a goal back before half-time, two goals by the prolific Bedford and another penalty by Angell saw QPR not only retain top spot in the league, but with 22 goals in just six games be the highest scorers in all four divisions.

An away win at Peterborough (Bedford scored his ninth goal of the season and it was only 8 September) was followed by the return match with Palace. Nearly 22,000 saw Palace shut out the potent QPR attack, the first time they had failed to score in 34 games. A single strike from Summersby condemned them to their first defeat of the season.

Next up were Barnsley, and despite winning 2-1 (both goals scored by Frank) and remaining top, they were jeered off the pitch at full time as the home fans were disappointed that Barnsley were not annihilated.

This indifferent performance was followed by two successive defeats, at home to Wrexham (whose goalkeeper Kevin Keelan made four outstanding saves against Frank) and away to Northampton. Frank was moved back to wing-half for the Northampton match and stayed there for the home League Cup defeat to Preston North End.

This was the last match QPR played at Loftus Road that season as refurbishments took place. The side played the rest of their home games at the world-famous White City Stadium, home to the Olympics, dog and speedway racing and athletics.

With Frank back up front for the visit to Southend, the team got back to winning ways with a convincing 3-1 victory, but a shattering 1-0 defeat at the White City for the first time, to Notts County, saw Alec Stock ring the changes.

Along with Roy Bentley and John Collins, Frank was dropped and missed the next four games, two defeats and two victories.

He returned to score in the FA Cup win over Newport County and starred in the impressive 4-2 away victory over Bristol Rovers. With the dodgy patch apparently over Reading were sent away 3-2 with Frank scoring the first and leading the line. A summary execution of non-league Hinckley Athletic, 7-2 in the next round of the FA Cup, was followed by two goalless draws against Shrewsbury and Millwall. Frank was dropped again while still adjusting to the new role of being the centre-forward and finding it difficult.

Recalled after a disappointing Christmas, Frank played his last league game for QPR in a humiliating 5-0 thrashing on 12 January at Swindon Town. The third round of the FA Cup (delayed because of the poor weather) was Frank's last game for Rangers, a feeble 2-0 defeat at Wrexham.

The promising start to the season had gone very sour. The wheels had come off and as Northampton stepped in to rescue Frank's season, QPR slipped steadily down the table to finish an exceptionally disappointing 13th. They failed to win any of their last eight games, losing six of them.

Seven goals in 22 starts was a fair return for a young man learning a new job and talking to him years later Frank told me that he admired Alec Stock greatly, a true gentleman and understood why he was dropped. The 'Welcome to London' had lasted for just six months and had been a steep learning curve, but it was a better experience than what was to follow when we returned in five and a half years' time.

Ironically Frank had applied to join 'The Rangers Club' on Ellersie Road, Shepherd's Bush. The entrance fee was a whopping £10 10 shillings, and the annual subscription the same. As a good Yorkshireman I hope he didn't pay up just as he was about to leave.

Frank Large's Queens Park Rangers record

	League		*FA Cup*		*League Cup*	
	Apps	Gls	Apps	Gls	Apps	Gls
1962/63	18	5	3	2	1	0

Total (all competitions): 22 appearances, 7 goals

5

Northampton I

FRANK Grande kindly sent me a seven-page letter detailing dad's three spells at the Cobblers, most of it paraphrased from his own excellent book published in 1997: *Northampton Town FC The Official History*. I have used this to form the backbone of his memorable spells at the club and I am deeply indebted to Frank and his wife Tina for their help and enthusiasm.

Frank Grande wrote, 'Cliff Holton had left the club. The man who had become the saviour of Northampton Town as the first post-war player to score a hat-trick on his debut was on his way.

'There was no disagreement or falling-out with the club, but he had business interests in North London and in his 15 months as a Cobbler he had worn out two cars running up and down from his London home.

'An unsuccessful bid for Cliff from Queens Park Rangers may have unsettled the out-and-out centre-forward, but Northampton manager Dave Bowen was not a man to despair – he was the type of manager who was always one step ahead, and while Cliff was packing his bags to join

Crystal Palace (the club he scored a hat-trick against on his Cobblers debut), Port Vale front-man Bert Llewellyn was on his way to the County Ground.

'The next game was against QPR at White City and the new buy lined up in the number nine shirt.

'There was a complete contrast between Holton and Llewellyn. Cliff stood over six feet tall, had a shot like a cannonball and was an out-and-out finisher. Bert stood 5ft 5ins but had the knack of being in the right place at the right time. Despite his small frame he was also good in the air.

'The match was full of incident. A drunk got on the pitch and attacked Cobblers duo Terry Branston and Theo Foley, who were trying to calm him down. Hell-bent on getting revenge for the Cobblers taking the lead, he then made a beeline for goalkeeper Chic Brodie – a big mistake!

'The Glaswegian custodian took the bottle off him and slammed him against the upright. It was one of the fastest sobering-up exercises ever seen as the drunk screamed to the on-rushing policeman to save him.

'The downside to the game was an injury to debutant Llewellyn after just 30 minutes. Sadly it proved to be long-term and he was not going to play again for some time.

'Sitting in the stand watching the game was a young forward who Rangers had bought from Halifax, and was struggling to keep his place on the starting panel. Dave Bowen made enquiries and by the middle of the week Frank Large was a Cobbler.'

Frank made his debut in front of nearly 19,000 people in a 0-0 draw with Coventry City on 2 March 1963. That was the winter that the game really froze. Despite the fact that he was in and out of the team at QPR, he hadn't played a match in over five weeks, and had made only five appearances in the previous two months.

The weather that winter played havoc with the fixtures. The third round of the FA Cup began on 5 January and was only fully completed on 11 March, with the final eventually being played on 25 May – three weeks later than usual.

This lack of fixtures maybe partly explains the high attendances as the bad weather receded, and Frank began to help Northampton's challenge for Third Division glory.

Frank Grande recalls the Coventry match, 'There were no goals in that game, but there were shades of what was to come as the club's new number nine hustled and bustled, chased and ran all over the field for a full 90 minutes.'

He continues, 'The blonde bomber opened his account at the next game against Bradford when he scored the first in a 3-1 win, and followed it up with a hat-trick in his next game at home to Colchester.'

With a house to sell in London and no home in Northampton, Mum and I stayed in the capital and Dad lived in 'digs' with two young apprentices, Graham Carr and Vic Cockroft.

Despite making over 90 appearances for the club and managing them to Fourth Division championship glory, Graham is probably more famous now as the father of top comedian Alan.

Graham recalls, 'You know that everybody liked your Dad. I've never in all my time in the game ever come across anybody who had a bad word to say about him.'

A nice start to our conversation as the ebullient Geordie gets into his stride. 'Do you remember that song?' he laughs and before I can say a word he launches into the first and only verse, 'He's here, he's there, he's every fucking where, Frankie Large, Frankie Large!'

Laughing, I remember that strange mix of pride and embarrassment as an eight-year-old sitting in the main stand as the Hotel End serenaded Frank with the simple song. My heart felt like it was fit to burst out of my chest. My brother and I were desperate to stand behind that goal and join in, but were forbidden by our Mum.

On match days we turned up an hour before kick-off and had the ground to ourselves. We always went to the Hotel End and stood looking up the pitch imagining we were there with the skinheads and 'hards' who chanted and adored Frank.

Graham clearly remembers Frank's first spell at the club. He was still a young trainee on the fringes of the first team and recalls that he didn't get many chances to play – his opportunity came later on, most notably a run of 27 games in the First Division as the Cobblers completed their only (to date) season in the top flight.

He says, 'We weren't allowed to go for a pint before the games, so on a Friday night we used to have a few beers in the digs – Watneys Pale Ale. Your Dad reckoned he needed it to settle his nerves and help him sleep, and me and Vic agreed! So anyway on the Saturday we'd go with the reserves, lose 3-0 and play like shite. Meanwhile your Dad's on the back page of the *Pink-un* having scored two amazing goals.'

He continues, 'Me and your Dad were best mates. I've a big glossy press photo of me and your Dad in a jazz club in Northampton in my scrapbook.'

A jazz club? I tell Graham that I didn't reckon that was my Dad's scene. 'Aye man your Dad was a pub man, he didn't like clubs, he liked men's company and was always happy watching a match.'

Not overly surprised by this summation garnered 40-plus years ago, I let Graham know that he never changed, happiest with a pint and a match on the telly, until the day he died.

Back to the 60s and the social life of the players at the club at the time.

Graham says, 'We didn't have too many good players at the club, but we had some great characters – Terry Branston for one, what a lad. Roly Mills used to look after the lottery and we used to go to the local pubs for that.'

Frank Grande recalls, 'The players were encouraged to go and play darts and skittles against the supporters. This bonding with the fans showed that the players were working class too, and not afraid to show it.'

As they weren't getting paid much more than the average industrial wage and egos were kept in check the players were not only approachable but were also appreciative and I reckon it's a fair point.

I ask Graham about Dave Bowen, and he replies, 'He was a fantastic manager, he did brilliantly on very limited resources, both going up and going down we were always the paupers.'

In the space of seven years Dave Bowen took Northampton Town from the Fourth Division to the First Division and back down again. The great Joe Mercer said, 'The miracle of 1966 wasn't England winning the World Cup, it was Northampton playing in the First Division.'

Graham adds, 'Dave Bowen always knew when we needed freshening up and his signings were generally good.' I agree knowing that he signed Frank on three separate occasions (February 1963, December 1966, and August 1969) and most pertinently only sold him once.

I remember asking Terry Branston, the big centre-half who played with Frank in his first two spells at the County Ground, about Bowen. 'Dave Bowen would soon have had you hung off the dressing room peg, if you weren't performing.' I asked him if he were a hard man. Terry laughed and answered diplomatically. 'Oh I thrived on it and so did your Dad.' I told him I knew that Frank had a lot of time for Dave Bowen. 'And Dave Bowen had a lot of time for your Dad.'

In the spring of 1963, 20 games had to be shoe-horned into less than 12 weeks as a result of the big freeze, and the season really took off. Frank Grande details the action, 'On the field Northampton were marching up the Third Division. Frank helped himself to another brace of goals to add to an Alec Ashworth hat-trick as the club stuck five past Reading. He also scored in both of the games versus Brighton that Easter, as did the Brighton centre-half Roy Jennings. Unfortunately for Roy his were own goals! In between those two games he scored the only goal in 1-0 victory over Shrewsbury and was almost averaging a goal a game.

'Another couple against Barnsley were followed by a 47-minute hat-trick against Southend in a thriller that saw the Cobblers win 5-3. It also saw Frank move past Cliff Holton's 14 goals to become the club's second top scorer.

'The icing on the cake came when he netted twice at home to Carlisle, assuring that the club won promotion to the Second Division for the first time in their history, as champions.

'Along with his medal (not engraved!), Frank also received a six-inch rubber Cobblers doll with blonde hair, blue eyes and number nine on the back.'

Theo Foley, the inspirational captain, recall to Frank Grande a story about how Frank raved about a local singer called Gerry Dorsey – in his opinion he was definitely on the way up.

Shortly after this revelation, according to Theo, Frank announced that the lad had changed his name to Englebert Humperdinck. This apparently brought howls of laughter in the dressing room and a fair bit of leg-pulling. Allegedly my Dad let it go over his head.

Then one day the singer was billed to appear at the ABC so a group of players attended and were unanimously impressed with the soon-to-be world superstar.

Having spoken to Frank Grande at length about writing a book, he mentioned that he found a lot of the ex-pros struggled to get the facts right and that memories were fading fast. I don't doubt Theo for one minute but I reckon that Frank, a Buddy Holly and Rolling Stones fan (and a former Teddy boy to boot) doesn't quite fit the identikit picture of an Englebert Humperdinck fan – but it's a good story.

The club's first ever game in the Second Division was an away win at Scunthorpe's Old Showgrounds. Frank scored along with Barry Lines in a 2-1 victory that was notable for the debut of club stalwart Joe Kiernan.

The resignation of Dave Bowen left the trainer Jack Jennings in temporary charge, and he did a great job notching three victories in his three matches. Despite a long list of willing replacements applying for the post his replacement was...Dave Bowen, who relented and returned to the job.

Despite losing 1-0 at home to Derby (their first home defeat in 23 matches) the side maintained a good mid-table position as they quickly found their feet in their new surroundings. One highlight was a 4-0 drubbing of Swindon (who had not lost all season), in which Frank scored two.

Three days later a young and soon-to-be famous Leeds United arrived at the County Ground and comfortably won 3-0. This was the first time that Frank had played against his home-town team. The second time procured a better result later that season, a 0-0 draw at Elland Road.

The programme notes that day commented, 'The Cobblers should be including that rare bird, a Leeds man playing against Leeds United – Frank Large, their big and lively forward from Halifax Town, whom we ourselves looked at quite a few times in his Shay days. This west Leeds man has notched nine goals already this season.'

Frank's final match against the team he supported all his life came in the top tier at Filbert Street in February 1968. Leicester City earned a deserved 2-2 draw with the title-chasing West Yorkshire outfit that contained ten full internationals.

It was the hapless Welsh goalkeeper Gary Sprake who gifted Frank probably the silliest goal of his career. A deep cross from the right wing saw Frank jump with the keeper just outside the six-yard box. Sprake, obviously disconcerted by Frank's presence, flapped and missed it completely. As they fell to the floor the ball rebounded off the far post and hit Frank's arse as he struggled to get up before trickling over the line, much to his amusement, and he proceeded to celebrate somewhat sheepishly. Due to the wonders of YouTube this is available in all its monochrome glory.

As the inaugural season in the new division stuttered along one incident stood out. During a dire 0-0 draw with Orient Frank suddenly felt a sharp pain in his back, and reaching round to investigate he pulled out a dart that had been thrown by a home supporter.

Apparently with little fuss the whole thing passed and the perpetrator was never found. Frank Grande wryly commented, 'It was the only shot on target all afternoon.'

A stunning 5-1 defeat of Sunderland as 1963 neared its end, on a frozen pitch, was achieved with the team opting to wear baseball boots purchased from the local sports store Bowen and Collins.

It was after a 3-2 defeat of Swindon, in which Frank scored, that Dave Bowen was made aware that Swindon manager Bert Head was interested in taking Frank south once again. Frank Grande relates that, 'Bowen always had a philosophy of moving forwards in and out of the club. During that season (1963/64) he used 26 players and half of them were forwards. John Reid and Roy Smith had moved to Luton, and Peter Kane was soon on his way to Crewe, while Billy Best, Tommy Robson, Jim Hall and Bobby Brown waited patiently in the wings.'

A fee of £10,000 was decided on and despite the fact that he was very happy at Northampton, Frank left for Swindon having agreed personal terms. The local paper reported, 'The club joker, the wise-cracking Frank Large had agreed terms and was leaving the Cobblers.'

Despite playing his last game for the club on 18 February his 12 goals in 29 starts saw him finish the season as Northampton's top scorer.

As for the Cobblers they finished the season in a very respectable 11th position, and the following year to universal astonishment secured promotion as runners-up to Newcastle United to the giddy heights of the First Division.

(Footnote: during our first stay in Northampton we lived in the leafy suburb of Duston, and 43 years later the town council named a road in a new development there Frank Large Way. Nice touch!!)

Frank Large's Northampton record

	League		*FA Cup*		*League Cup*	
	Apps	*Gls*	*Apps*	*Gls*	*Apps*	*Gls*
1962/63	20	18	0	0	0	0
1963/64	27	12	1	0	1	0

Total (all competitions): 49 appearances, 30 goals

6

Swindon Town

IT was significant that in the two matches Frank had played against Swindon that season, he had scored three goals, two in a barnstorming performance at the end of September that saw Swindon's ten-match unbeaten run come to an end as the Cobblers put four past them at the County Ground, Northampton.

It had obviously impressed the Swindon manager Bert Head, who contacted Dave Bowen to discuss Frank's availability. The fee was agreed but the whole deal depended upon whether Bobby Hunt would leave Colchester to join the Cobblers. He did and despite late complications that saw Bowen hesitate, Frank felt that the move was right and off we all went (four of us now as our Richard was born in Northampton in November of 1963).

Coincidently our David was also born in Northampton during Frank's second term at the club in 1967 and Vicky in 1970 in his third spell! We got good value out of the Barret Maternity Hospital.

Within an hour of signing for Swindon the club was thrown into crisis by the shock transfer request of star left-half Bobby Woodruff, who wanted the chance to play in the top flight. He left for Wolverhampton Wanderers for a fee of £35,000, then a club record for Swindon.

It had been a busy week for Bert who had also signed Hartlepool United's goalkeeper Norman Oakley two days previous for £7,000.

Frank made his debut on 7 March 1964, coincidently his 200th league game, at home to Plymouth Argyle, scoring both goals in a 2-1 victory. Tactically Swindon got it right against an Argyle side packing their defence as they fought off relegation.

Roger Malone wrote in the *Pink-un*, 'No Swindon youngster would have scored. He is essentially a smash-and-grab scorer who scrambles close range goals amongst a tangle of flailing legs and bodies. There are many more of that kind to be got in the Second Division than there are spectacular goals. Two such untidy goals decided this game.'

Bert Head was more fulsome in his praise. 'Frankie Large played as I anticipated he would. Although life was made difficult with a packed defence he still showed plenty of enthusiasm and good honest endeavour. Always a danger in the six-yard box, he snapped up his two goals to make his debut first class. He is a real harasser and given the opportunity can take goals quite well in the air.'

Another player who made a significant contribution that day was Mike Summerbee, the future Manchester City and England star. He was moved from the wing to inside-left where he added 'a fighting spirit to the scheming operations behind the front line'. I remember Dad telling me that he got on well with Mike and that he complemented his play, describing him as 'a great crosser of the ball perfect for centre-forwards'. He took a great interest in Mike's future career and was delighted he did so well.

A goal in a 2-2 draw at Charlton secured only the second away point of the season – it was 14 March – and a subsequent 2-0 home victory over Middlesbrough was only the second win in 14 games.

A crowd of 22,096 turned up to see the Robins take on Cardiff City, with the great John Charles at centre-half. The fact that Frank managed a goal brings great pleasure, but unfortunately it wasn't enough as Cardiff managed two of their own.

Five defeats in the last six games of the season condemned the side to 14th place in the league, the last match a humiliating 5-1 thrashing at Southampton in which the soon-to-be Spurs favourite Martin Chivers scored a hat-trick. Frank failed to register in these last six games and finished that season with four goals in ten matches for Swindon.

The new campaign started in a similar vein with a humiliating 6-1 demolition away at Bury. It surely didn't help that the goalkeeper Oakley was carried off injured after only six minutes.

Despite starting the first seven games of the season (which saw three home victories, one home defeat and three away defeats) Frank failed to score and his manager decided it might be time to move him on. A poor return of just four goals in 17 matches (all of which were scored in his first four games) meant that when Carlisle United showed some interest his value had fallen from ten grand to £6,500.

I asked Frank once about his comparative lack of success in the south (QPR, Swindon and Fulham) and he told me he felt that his style of hustle and bustle wasn't appreciated as much – by either the players or the fans.

He also told me that they appeared to be reluctant to get the ball into the box early and therefore didn't play to his strengths. He felt that the fans would get on his back, and he hated that, as he always tried so hard.

Frank didn't remember his time fondly at Swindon and was frustrated at his lack of goalscoring, but he didn't have to worry for long as a new and successful challenge lay just around the corner.

Swindon continued to struggle all season and paid the ultimate price by finishing in 21st place and suffering relegation to the Third Division.

Frank Large's Swindon Town record

	League		*FA Cup*		*League Cup*	
	Apps	*Gls*	*Apps*	*Gls*	*Apps*	*Gls*
1963/64	10	4	0	0	0	0
1964/65	7	0	0	0	0	0

Total (all competitions): 17 appearances, 4 goals

7

Carlisle United

CARLISLE'S interest was confirmed one day in the second week of September when Frank turned up for training and was told that Swindon had agreed a fee with the Cumbrians and that all he had to do was agree personal terms.

Easier said than done! It is 250 miles from Wiltshire to Cumberland, but in those days it was a daunting six-hour drive. Unperturbed and keen to get away he drove to Carlisle to meet the manager Alan Ashman, signed, then drove back to tell Mum.

Carlisle had been promoted from the Fourth Division the previous season, just missing out on the top spot, and with 39 goals boasted the league's top scorer Hugh McIlmoyle.

Just three days younger than Frank, McIlmoyle's career shared a number of remarkable similarities. As goalscorers, both were involved in numerous transfers – unusual in those days – and both had three spells at a club (McIlmoyle had three stints with Carlisle) which is rare in any career, but for both to do it with unfashionable clubs who climbed from the lowest tier to the top and back again is surely unique.

Carlisle's form so far that season was mixed with only one victory in their first six games. Frank made his debut on 26 September in a 4-3 home defeat to Bournemouth (they were 3-2 up at half-time). Ashman initially sought to pair him up front with McIlmoyle, who had been struggling recently in front of goal, and in Frank's first six games for the club it was McIlmoyle who wore the number nine shirt. It took McIlmoyle's departure to First Division side Wolverhampton Wanderers, for a club record fee of £30,000, to kick-start the season.

Another piece of shrewd business was completed that October when Willie Carlin, a small Liverpudlian with a big heart and good engine, was bought from Halifax Town. A tenacious player, Carlin not only helped make goals, he also scored his fair share as well. Alex South felt that Willie had the same attitude to the game as Frank and he told me, 'Willie never gave up, he always fought to the end, and that lifted you.'

With Frank now partnering another Scouser, Johnny Evans, the side set off on an unbeaten run of six matches, winning four of them. Unfortunately this run came to a spectacular end in the first round of the FA Cup away to non-league Crook Town. Another 1-0 defeat to Southend a week later saw them wedged behind the leaders in a league that no one team dominated.

By this time we had all settled into a club house in Carlisle and it was officially the coldest house we ever lived in (and we lived in a number of houses!). We used to go to bed in woolly jumpers, hats and gloves, with hot water bottles and as many blankets as Mum could find!

I got to speak to Peter McConnell, the club captain, and we had a long and entertaining conversation in which he reminisced about that season many years ago. He told me that he had co-authored a book, *Nice One Skip,* with Andy Hall, the media officer of Carlisle United, and that there were a few anecdotes concerning Frank.

Softly-spoken with a voice that belies his age, Peter called Frank the 'Human Bulldozer', and in the book says, 'He was a player who had a huge heart. The crowd loved him for that because he gave us everything, and he was never one to hide away. We all knew the drill; if you had the ball and you didn't have anywhere else to go, you simply hung it up and dropped it into the box. Big Frank did the rest for you. Either the ball, the keeper or both would end up in the back of the net, with Frank steaming through everything in his path to get the final touch on it.'

A 4-1 thrashing of Colchester at Brunton Park on 12 December, in which Frank scored two, was followed by a 6-1 thumping away at Brentford – hardly the form of promotion challengers, let alone champions. This was Frank's 246th match in the Football League and his goal was his 100th.

Ashman's last foray in the transfer market that season saw Ronnie Simpson, a local lad who had played all his football in Yorkshire, join Carlisle from Sheffield United. An experienced left-winger, he quickly established himself in the first team, providing invaluable service to the top two.

Two 1-0 victories over local rivals Workington on 26 and 28 December (Frank scored at home, Peter McConnell away) saw 1964 end with the team nicely placed for a promotion challenge in the New Year. However the visit of league leaders Bristol Rovers on 2 January showed how far off the chase they were as they suffered a 2-1 defeat that dampened the New Year celebrations.

Then a run of five straight victories, beginning with Grimsby Town at home and followed by three wins at Oldham Athletic, Scunthorpe United and Bournemouth and a home victory over Peterborough saw the team maintain their momentum as the new league leaders Hull City arrived at Brunton Park on 20 February.

The club's biggest crowd since 1956, 17,174, saw a 0-0 draw that the local reporter David Steele wrote a lovely article about:

'Hull at that time were experiencing something of a boom aided by the wealth of chairman Harold Needler. They were the new leaders of the division and were attracting crowds of over 25,000 to Boothferry Park. Peter McConnell told me that they found out that the Hull players were on massive bonuses to get promotion. This apparently annoyed Stan Harland so much that he went to see the chairman and the manager to get an increase on the meagre sums on offer at Brunton Park. Frustrated at the lack of progress he grabbed the chairman by his tie! No record exists that this tactic worked, but it certainly got them nowhere near the £1,000 that Peter reckoned the Hull players were on.'

Although Carlisle failed to score for the first time in ten matches so did Hull, who had a late goal disallowed. Despite losing unexpectedly to Gillingham, successive home victories against Scunthorpe (3-1) and Exeter City (2-1) saw them travel to Loftus Road to meet a struggling QPR side. Trailing 1-0 at half-time in front of a miserly crowd of just 5,934, Carlisle turned it around in the second half with goals by Blain and Evans to go top of the table – a position they never relinquished.

The run-in saw them win five out of seven games, one of which was at Reading with goals from the two Scouse jokers Evans and Carlin. Peter remembers that night before, 'Willie [Carlin] and Johnny [Evans] used to room together on our away trips, and they were the cause of all kinds of trouble with their wind-ups and antics. My room-mate for the trip to Reading was Frank Large, who didn't suffer fools lightly at all, and there was one night when he was pushed to boiling point by our resident jokers, despite the fact that they were actually innocent on this occasion.

'We were in a hotel not far from Reading…and Frank had left his shoes in the corridor for the porter to clean. Once he got himself ready he stuck his head outside the door to get them and started ranting and swearing when he spotted they weren't there. He immediately went along the corridor and banged on their door, demanding that they hand the shoes over immediately. The lads told him they had no idea what he was on about, but Frank was having none of it. He thumped the door harder, and gave them an ultimatum – shoes back or else. Again they told him to go away (it sounded like that anyway) and that left Frank with steam rising out of his ears.

'The red mist descended and the next thing I saw was big Frank on the floor in their room, with splinters all around him, and the remains of the door hanging off the hinges. At almost that exact moment the porter came around the corner and walked up to Frank, handed him the missing items and said, "Your shoes sir", before quickly heading off to get the hotel manager. We were asked to pack up and leave about 20 minutes later, and it took a while for the three of them to see the funny side.'

The final two games that season, as was the norm in those days, were back-to-back matches, and as fate would have it Carlisle's opponents Mansfield Town were also in the hunt for the ultimate prize.

On Easter Monday they travelled to Field Mill (where Mansfield were undefeated since October) and were soundly beaten 2-0. Despite this defeat they still had their destiny in their own hands – a win in the last game of the season would secure the championship.

The return match was played the very next day and 18,764 people were packed in to the ground, with thousands locked outside, on 20 April 1965. Everything hinged on the last 90 minutes of the season – if Mansfield won they could be crowned champions and Carlisle could miss out on promotion.

Having placed a small article in the *Cumberland News* (with the help of Phil Rostron) looking for memories of Frank's year at Carlisle, a number of fans got in touch. Most eloquent was a message from Warwick Sloane, a native of Carlisle now living in Edinburgh, who along with a lovely letter sent actual footage of the final game of that momentous season. His letter read:

> 'Dear Paul
> 'Although this package arrives to you from Edinburgh, I am a native of Carlisle and indeed still own a house there. A lifelong United supporter, I can recall with fondness

the club's best period, circa: 1963 to 1975. Ensconced within that time-frame is a fervent remembrance of your father's contribution in the 1964/65 season when we reached the dizzy and unprecedented heights of Third Division champions.

'Needing to beat second-placed Mansfield at Brunton Park on the final day of the season, fearless Frank grabbed a brace and was actually denied a hat-trick when hitting a post.

'Thirty years after that memorable evening I recalled that the game was committed to posterity by Border TV cameras and so it was on a whim in 1995 I sent an impassioned plea to their studios in the hope of procuring a copy. To their eternal credit they forwarded extant footage while admitting that much of the transmission could not be salvaged. Hence you'll please find enclosed the salient moments on the video which captures your dad's goals on that night.

'Incidently the commentary is by one Derek Batey who years later gained considerable fame by hosting a TV programme named *Mr and Mrs.*

'Another video in my collection shows the Mansfield game at greater length and your dad is featured throughout, there is even a sequence depicting him off field and at his leisure with fellow forwards Evans (now deceased) and Carlin.

'Although you may have a legion of action photos, may I strongly recommend a snap taken by the *Cumberland News*, the same journal that featured your request. They own the copyright to a stunning picture of the first goal versus Mansfield. Your father is airborne in a jack-knife position and appears to have attained a remarkable height.

'You certainly open the floodgates of memory with reference to the name FRANK LARGE. Were there a top ten table of "have boots will travel", Frank would receive my nomination for top spot! In a remarkable career covering Swindon, Fulham, Carlisle, Leicester, Leeds, QPR and Northampton this begs the question, how did your mother cope with such a nomadic lifestyle? She must have seen a goodly number of removal vans in her time!

'These transfers stemmed from his hard-earned reputation as a proven goalscorer at every club he graced. You may be familiar with his tally up and down the land, I haven't the figures to hand but I have seen the statistics in the past and they were astonishing!

'With some irony, the last decent soccer book I read was Sir Bobby Robson's autobiography and your dad is mentioned in glowing terms appertaining to his Fulham career.

'Looking back on it, Frank must have been incredibly fit. At one Brunton Park encounter he powered a shot in at one end of the pitch and when the opposition counter-attacked there he was heading a goal-bound effort off his own goal line. He gave value for money and paying spectators appreciated his lion-hearted exertions.

'I was saddened and not a little shocked when my sister rang to tell me of your dad's demise. If my memory is to be trusted, that would be about August 2003, when in his 63rd year.

'Plenty of material for a book which your father does deserve and to that end I hope that good fortune attends all your future endeavours. Your manuscript should meet with universal approval when bearing in mind all the soccer outposts he attended. He must have near legendary status in Northampton for starters.

'As a postscript, you may not be aware that Frank along with another player, Joe Livingstone, spent the out-of-season months working for the Carlisle Brewery. In essence, this involved delivery of casks to all the city hostelries, which at that time were under state management. A pleasant enough way to pass the summer of 1965 with plenty of fine ale as a perk of the job.

'If I can be of further assistance I am at your disposal.

'Every best wish

'From

Warwick Sloane'

The film shows the ground fit to bursting, the big old stand with the massive advert for Senior Service Cigarettes on its roof full to overflowing. An impossibly flimsy wooden fence guarding the playing surface looks ready to throw in the towel at any moment.

Just before kick-off a besuited man, bedecked in his club scarf runs on to the pitch and places what looks like a stuffed dog on the centre circle. It is not a dog but a fox named Olga and the tradition is in honour of Cumberland's most famous son John Peel, the hunter – not the Liverpool-loving, sadly deceased DJ.

With the formalities over the game commences, and Frank's first touch (not surprisingly a header) flashes just wide. Then the right-winger Jimmy Blain roars past the hapless right-back and crosses perfectly for Frank to rise and nod the ball in for 1-0 after 14 minutes. A still photo from another angle shows him twisting in a jack-knife position to power the ball past the keeper.

Blain sets up the second with another inviting cross that Frank gets on the end of, to send an arcing header over the advancing keeper. To me it looks like it's going in, but just to make sure Johnny Evans arrives and makes sure from all of a yard for 2-0. When I ask Peter he agrees that it was really Frank's goal.

On 35 minutes a long ball is missed by the Mansfield centre-half and quick as a flash Frank tamely taps it home (courtesy of his shinbone) via the post for 3-0, game over.

The highlights show next to nothing of the second half and miss a stunning strike that would have secured the hat-trick Frank deserved.

Thankfully it was recorded the day after the game in *The Journal*, 'The crowd who had plenty to cheer suddenly gasped as Large swung his right foot fully 40 yards from goal, and the ball flew like an arrow to quiver a post and come out before the keeper shaped.'

As the match approaches the 90th minute the reporter Ivor Broadis finishes his report thus, 'Socks down, shin guards discarded, United played out time as the spectators scorned the barriers to line the touchlines. It was over, a magnificent end to a hard season.'

The pitch invasion was spontaneous and joyous, ending a 60-year wait for Second Division football. As the players sipped champagne in the directors' box Alan Ashman was quoted as saying, 'I was over the moon when we were promoted into the Third Division last season, but tonight I think I am the proudest and happiest man in football. We have been inspired right through the season by a wonderful band of supporters, this is a great and wonderful day for Carlisle.'

Frank's contribution was 16 goals in 38 games to secure his second Third Division championship medal in two years. The celebrations continued long into the night and I have some lovely photos of the players sipping champagne in Babycham glasses while being swamped by supporters and officials alike, on the pitch, in the changing room and eventually in the bath!

Peter McConnell had an eventful night, losing his mother along the way as the lads set off to enjoy themselves, and he recalls, 'We were all soon suited and booted and heading towards town. It was a fantastic night, it really was, as the whole of Carlisle seemed to be out and about and the place was buzzing with excitement.'

Carlisle had finished as champions with 60 points, one ahead of both Bristol City and Mansfield, and just two ahead of Hull in fourth. To highlight just how tight the division was that season, Gillingham finished in seventh, only five points behind Carlisle.

Interviewed many years later for a club programme, McConnell summed up the occasion well, 'That last match of the season when we beat Mansfield 3-0 was the highlight of my career here. We had some good cup ties in my time but never a game like this one, you couldn't script a situation like it, nobody could have lived with us that night… the scenes at the end were unbelievable and it still makes my hair stand on end to think about it.'

An official reception and dinner took place five days later in Carlisle's Gretna Ballroom to commemorate the success. The right worshipful the Mayor of Carlisle, Alderman Howard Glaister JP, requested the company of Mr and Mrs Frank Large. I am sure they had a good night!

As was the norm in the close-season at the time, the clubs reduced the players' wages and they were encouraged to go and work for local businesses. Dad and Joe Livingstone, as mentioned by Warwick, landed on their feet, getting a job with the Carlisle Brewery, delivering casks of the local brew to the town and surrounding village pubs. One perk of the job was a free glass of ale for every delivery – no surprise that it was one of the best jobs he ever had. The other event of note that summer was our first visit to Mum's family in Westport, Co Mayo, Republic of Ireland. Mum and Dad, me and our kid, Grandma and Granddad and uncle Dermot all travelled over in Dad's gorgeous black MK2 Jaguar.

Peter recalls that Frank used to enjoy driving that car fast and had more than his fair share of near misses as they used to take it in turns to drive to training.

'One week we were going down Moorhouse Hill past the Museum pub and down into the dip, when the bonnet of his car popped up and flew off. There was no warning or anything like that, it was just whoosh, and it was gone. It whipped over our heads, missing us by inches and landed about 20 to 30 yards behind us. Thank heavens there was nobody following behind because it would have done them some serious injury.

'Not to give too much away but it's a safe bet to say that we were probably doing about 80mph as we set off down that hill, because that's how Frank liked to drive. I just sat there and shook my head at him as he grinned back at me with a ridiculous smile that covered most of his face.'

The new season began with a thumping 4-1 defeat of Norwich at home. Frank scored one and Willie Carlin's replacement Chris Balderstone got another. Chris went on to become both a footballing and cricketing legend, one of the last professionals who succeeded at both codes.

Four wins in the first six games showed that Carlisle could hold their own in the league, but eight games without a goal meant that Frank was struggling. He once told me that when a barren spell happened he used to get his head down, work harder and believe in himself, knowing it would turn around.

However in this instance it was Alan Ashman who took control. Frank being dropped for the month of December took its toll on their relationship, and when Oldham manager Gordon Hurst made an offer of £8,000 both parties were happy to part ways.

I was contacted by a friend of Frank's from that time, former policeman Bob Taylor, who not only regaled me with stories of the pubs the players used to frequent, but also with an interesting anecdote about his departure.

Bob was on foot patrol when Frank pulled up in the Jag (unbelievably he could still remember the number plate 44 years later). He told him that he'd had a massive bust-up with Ashman and asked for a transfer. Whether he did or not, that Christmas saw us move to Oldham and Frank made his debut on New Year's Day 1966.

Frank Large's Carlisle United record

	League		*FA Cup*		*League Cup*	
	Apps	*Gls*	*Apps*	*Gls*	*Apps*	*Gls*
1964/65	36	16	1	0	1	0
1965/66	14	2	0	0	1	0

Total (all competitions): 53 appearances, 18 goals

8

Oldham Athletic

PHIL Rostron, an ardent Oldham fan and renowned journalist, remembers:

'Going to the Latics became a lifetime habit for me after I first ventured to Boundary Park, a three-mile walk from my home in Shaw to watch a Third Division (North) game against Rochdale in late 1958. I was seven-and-a-half years old and something happened on that Saturday afternoon to hook me into an eternal love affair.

'I liked the way Peter Phoenix, Oldham's half-back, constantly ran with the ball from midfield, looking to feed John Bazley on the wing or Bert Lister, the centre-forward. The roar of the crowd was something I'd never heard before and I couldn't take my eyes off the man who walked around the entire periphery of the playing area at half-time with a tray of sweets to buy.

'The match ended 0-0 and with just one match to play Oldham were to finish 15th in a table topped by Scunthorpe United.

'All fairly unremarkable stuff, but for this seven-year-old a magical world had been discovered.

'This walk in the company of older boys like Keith Whitehead, Fred Claber and Alec Reekie to and from a place that was to become my shrine quickly became a compulsion. If the Latics were playing we were walking to watch them.

'Much had to be explained to me by my more senior fans. The structure of the Football League was to change over the coming summer, with the disbanding of the Third Division (North) and Third Division (South) and the introduction of four divisions.

'Oldham Athletic were to be in the Fourth Division and more exotic names than Rochdale were to visit Boundary Park. Goodness me we were to have Crystal Palace, Northampton and Torquay and the likes.

'I learned about promotion and relegation and a new puzzle was presented when it came to the FA Cup. Oldham were drawn at home in the second round to South Shields and were expected to beat them, it was revealed because they were a non-league side. They duly did.

'My Christmas presents that year, besides the obligatory tangerine, were a blue and white knitted scarf and a noisy wooden rattle, known locally as a "ricker". This was duly painted blue and white and proudly carried to matches to add to the din.

'Soon I learned a terrace song:

"We are supporters of The Latics
"Jack Rowley is our king
"John McCue is our left full-back
"Bob Ledger is the wizard of the wing
"John Bollands is our goalie

"Bobby Johnstone inside-right
"Bert Lister is the crasher
"For the boys in blue and white."

'Come 1965 and big changes were afoot at Oldham Athletic. Ken Bates became chairman just before the turn of the year at a time when there was a significant gap between home fixtures. After the 2-2 draw with Bournemouth on 11 December, Boundary Park was to fall still and silent until New Year's Day, when Shrewsbury were the visitors. As the Latics took to the field they were not in the old blue and white with which we had become so familiar but in electric orange shirts and shocking blue shorts. There were gasps in awe.

'Further, the team line-up featured no fewer than five new faces with the likes of Ian Towers, Reg Bloor and one Frank Large. It had been deemed that Oldham's main failing was a lack of goals and much faith was being placed in the new number nine, a thick-set hulk of a man with striking blond hair.

'They say that in life in general it takes only a matter of seconds to know whether or not you will get along with a stranger introduced to you. From the moment Frank Large chased his first ball in Oldham's gaudy colours I knew a special player-fan bond was sealed on the spot. I recall Oldham attacking the Rochdale Road end in the first half and an over-hit pass from midfield that would have been given up as a lost cause by 99 per cent of players was chased right to its exit from the playing area by the industrious Large.

'Combative, daring and full of energy, he was certainly my man of the match in a game lost 1-0, but which nevertheless held much promise.

'In the summer of 1966 England was spellbound as its national footballers plotted their way to the World Cup. Geoff Hurst may have scored a never-to-be-forgotten hat-trick, but that was as nothing compared to the prospect of seeing big Frank in action for Oldham in the coming months.

'With Large at the spearhead Oldham were rampant on home territory, beating Leyton Orient 3-1, Swansea and Shrewsbury both 4-1, Bristol Rovers 3-0, Walsall 6-2, Scunthorpe 2-0, Torquay 5-0 and Darlington 4-0.

'Frankie was lapping it up. And so was I along with several thousand others who had taken him to their hearts. We loved his non-stop running, his constant threat in the box and his propensity for scoring goals with anything but his foot. They'd go in off his head, his shoulder, his stomach, his knee. One went in off his backside. But all the while he was racking up the goals and revelling in his role of terrace idol.

'One terrace companion once said to me, "If they opened the gate at the back of the Chedderton Road End, he'd sure as hell run through it."

'Then when 18 goals in 34 games had been his far from inconsiderable contribution, the unthinkable happened.

'It was announced, to my utter dismay and complete disgust, that my hero was being sold to Northampton Town, from whence he had come via Swindon Town and Carlisle United.

'I was apoplectic to the point that I wrote a letter to Bates and initiated a two-juvenile protest march with my pal Peter Challinor on the Oldham Athletic offices in Sheepfoot Lane.

'The march was to no avail but I did receive a two page A4 letter from the chairman explaining that the bid they had received from Northampton was too good to turn down and an assurance that he would be replaced by a better quality centre-forward.

'The first point was difficult to argue with, the second an affront. There wasn't a better centre-forward in England, Europe or the world than Frank Large!

'I got to speak to my hero just once. Meeting the team bus, I waited for him to step on to the pavement before telling him enthusiastically, "Frank, you're fantastic."

'He grinned and replied, "So the missus keeps telling me."

'More than half a century on from my first visit, I still watch and support Oldham Athletic. Centre-forwards have come and centre-forwards have gone. Many of them.

'None can hold a candle to "the blonde bomber" who lit up a little boy's life.'

Frank Large's Oldham Athletic record

	League		*FA Cup*		*League Cup*	
	Apps	*Gls*	*Apps*	*Gls*	*Apps*	*Gls*
1965/66	18	7	2	0	0	0
1966/67	16	11	1	1	0	0

Total (all competitions): 37 appearances, 19 goals

9

Northampton II

FOLLOWING Frank's transfer to Swindon Town in February 1964 the Cobblers had finished a respectable 11th in a division that saw Leeds United and Sunderland promoted to the top flight.

The 1964/65 season resulted in promotion, a point behind champions Newcastle United, anchored by a run of 17 games undefeated, underpinned by a back four of Branston, Lock, Foley and Everitt that remained relatively unchanged all season. Seven penalty saves by Brian Harvey also helped. He even saved two in the same game against Southampton from the legendary Terry Paine, who was England's penalty taker at the time!

Promotion was achieved at Gigg Lane as Bury were buried 4-0. The result was marred by the sad news that chairman Fred York had died, never getting to see his team in the top division.

The club's only season (to date) at the highest level saw them maintain a good home record, including notable victories over Leeds, Newcastle and West Ham, but shocking away form made it an uphill struggle.

Frank Grande recalls how the 'wonder year' ended: 'It all came to a head in the penultimate game of the season against Fulham on 23 April 1966. In front of another record crowd of 24,423 and with the Cobblers 2-1 up, the Fulham goalkeeper fumbled the ball on the goal line, and as the supporters rose as one to celebrate not just a win and two points but possible salvation – no whistle, no goal! Joe Kiernan looked to the referee and later says, "I turned to the referee Jack Taylor, but he pointed to the linesman, who had fallen over, and was in no position to see the goal. Sorry Joe I can't give it, sorry."

'Fulham subsequently scored three and while it didn't result in automatic relegation, it did mean that survival was out of Northampton's hands. Victory over Sunderland was followed by a 3-0 defeat at Blackpool and relegation. They finished in 21st position, just two points behind Fulham and safety.'

Despite initially retaining most of the team who struggled so hard to stay in the First Division, and attempting to secure new signings (including Mike O'Grady from Leeds United) the new season began badly.

The loss of key players to injuries, and the transfers of both the previous season's top scorers (Hudson to Tranmere Rovers and Brown to Cardiff City) didn't help. Another factor must have been the fact that most of the players had been on an emotional and physical rollercoaster for six consecutive seasons of constant promotion and relegation battles.

Manager Dave Bowen felt that the only way to survive was to bring in not just a proven goalscorer, but a player who could change a side's fortunes. Frank was one such player with his infectious energy, enthusiasm and never-say-die attitude bringing out the best in the men around him.

Bowen wasn't the only manager to appreciate this ability, and it's no surprise or coincidence that seven of Frank's ten transfers took place in the mid-season with the teams concerned either fighting for promotion or against relegation.

His positive influence on the pitch was also appreciated off it. Terry Branston, who played with Frank during his first two spells with Northampton, remembered him fondly, 'We'd played up north somewhere, and we were queuing up to get into a club when the doorman comes up and tells us it was full. Well your Dad was having none of that and he goes up to this fella and says: "Do you know who I am ? I'm Frank Large…blah de blah!" Well it worked and we all got in.

'Superb, he had that bit of charisma about him, didn't he? For me he'd be the one you wanted with you if you were in the trenches. If you could pick someone to be with you when the going got tough I'd have Frank Large every time. Oh yes, your Dad was a character.'

I ask Terry what he was like to play against and he struggled to remember that when he was at Lincoln they played Northampton in February 1972 at the County Ground, winning 3-2.

Then the penny drops, 'He was a handful, tough and hard, but fair, and because we were mates we had a laugh.'

I mention that the game saw the end of Graham Taylor's playing career. 'Oh yes, he played full-back,' replies Terry. He tells me that he could have got the manager's job at Lincoln that year, but he didn't put in for it, and it was Taylor – then aged just 28 – who took his first step on the managerial ladder.

I took the opportunity to ask Terry about Frank's nemesis, the Coventry City centre-half George Curtis, whom he played against on nine occasions, failing to score and winning only once.

'He wasn't that big, but strong, strong as a blooming ox and very useful. A good club man and that's what it's all about. I remember your Dad getting injured by George and refusing to come off at half-time – saying he had unfinished business, with hindsight he should have.'

Frank was quoted in an Oldham Athletic programme in March 2001 for a game against Northampton Town, in an interview under the heading 'Goalden Boys', as saying, 'The toughest defender, Coventry's George Curtis, would kick you from start to finish. I remember one day he stooped to head the ball, and I gave him such a crack in retribution for what he'd done to me. But he simply got up and carried on as if nothing had happened.

'Later he kneed me in the back and it left me with a lump the size of a goldfish bowl, which eventually required an operation.'

Before the operation, during the season the fluid used to be drained regularly by hypodermic needle! As Terry said, 'It was a man's game.'

I contacted George, via Coventry City, and got a lovely polite letter saying that while he remembered the name, his memory wasn't so good any more and he couldn't recollect playing against Frank.

As for Terry I had the pleasure and honour of meeting him on several occasions and enjoyed his company immensely. He was a true gentleman who sadly passed away in 2010.

So Dave Bowen offered Ken Bates £15,000 – which he accepted unhesitatingly – for Dad's services and as Christmas 1966 approached we moved into a club house, 230 Hazeldine Road on the Links estate, and so began our second spell in Northampton.

Frank's debut in a 3-0 defeat by Birmingham City on Boxing Day was not the most auspicious (it also marked his 300th league game), but revenge was to come quickly. As was the way in those days, back-to-back fixtures saw Birmingham travel to Northampton the very next day, and he scored in a 2-1 win.

Maurice Weedon, writing in the *Soccer Star* in January 1967, noted, 'Northampton too near the bottom of the Second Division for comfort, last month signed centre-forward Frank Large from Oldham, their offer of £15,000 topping the bid made by Bristol Rovers who are also involved in the Second Division relegation battle.

'When Dave Bowen needed a player to boost his attack and heard that Large was for transfer he remembered what a grand 90-minute player Large was and moved in quickly to sign him. Northampton have always been a happy club and Large was delighted at re-joining his former club.

'He got off to a great start by scoring the winning goal against Birmingham in his first home game, and what is even more important, he brought zip and dash to an attack that has been inept all season. He followed that by netting the winner in a 2-1 away win over Rotherham. Against the Millers the whole side seemed to catch Large's enthusiasm and gave their finest display of the season.'

However a six-match run without a victory saw the team drop into the relegation zone and despite encouraging victories over Cardiff and Huddersfield, squandering a 3-0 lead at home to Carlisle summed up the season which saw them relegated for the second successive year.

Sadly Frank's impact wasn't enough. They had 13 points after 21 games when he arrived, and managed just 17 from the remaining 21 games, with Frank scoring eight times.

The most immediate impact was Dave Bowen's decision to move upstairs to become general manager/secretary, while Tony Marchi, the former Tottenham half-back, took over as manager. However he was unable to buy any new players until the wage bill was cut, and he had to make a list of players 'open to offers'.

Frank wasn't on the list but was the first to move when Leicester came in with a bid of £20,000. The offer was good for both the player and the club.

Frank Grande remembers the last home game in that second spell at the Cobblers, a game that 'would live forever in his memory, and the memory of many supporters who saw the game. It was against Bristol Rovers who were struggling. They had to play part-time defender and veteran Ray Mabbutt at centre-forward, because of injuries.

'Frank opened the scoring as he ploughed through the County Ground mud to give the Cobblers the lead, but Rovers were soon level after Harvey could only parry a shot to the feet of Mabbutt.

'Northampton were back in front when Frank was bundled over in the box and John Mackin converted the penalty. It was ex-Cobbler Bobby Jones, now back as a Rovers player, who equalised for a second time. It was his first for a year, his last effort was for the Cobblers at the County Ground.

'Rovers then went in front via a 30-yard effort, but that man Frank netted his second of the game to make it 3-3, and all before half-time.

'Late in the second half the scoring started again, Mabbutt scoring his second with a simple tap-in, then the score evened out again when our man netted his hat-trick. Minutes later Mabbutt completed a similar feat as Rovers ran out 5-4 victors.

'A very select band of players have scored a hat-trick and finished on the losing side, just another record in an eventful career.'

It was possibly this performance that clinched Matt Gillies's decision to take Frank to Leicester City and the First Division.

According to Graham Carr it certainly wasn't his next match, away to Barrow, his last in his second spell, and 100th appearance for the Cobblers.

Graham recalls, 'Me and your Dad had a few beers that Friday night before the game, no we weren't pissed or anything, just a few, three or four, no more. You see Marchi had lost the dressing room, and with your Dad leaving we felt we could have a beer, and we didn't care. Anyway as I said we got beat 4-0 and if Matt Gillies had been watching him that day he wouldn't have signed him!"

He reminisces some more, 'I missed him loads when he left, he was me best mate, he'd be the first out of the shower, towel down his hair and be ready to go. After training it was Bob's Cafe, and after a match it was the Old Black Lion, down by the railway station, as some of the younger lads had digs down there and a lot of them didn't have cars. Your Dad had a green mini-van and off he'd go, I still laugh thinking about it, the height of him and his fucking knees and elbows over the steering wheel. He was a fantastic laugh, we had some great times, he was brilliant was your Dad.'

I ask Graham about the Sunday dinnertime session in the pub up the road from us in Hazeldine Road. Frank's ritual was to get up and read the paper, go to the pub, come home, have his Yorkshire puddings and gravy, followed by the roast beef and veg – and then a good kip.

'Oh, Jesus, The Pioneer, yeah a few of us would go in on a Sunday with your Dad and Crutch [John Kurilla] and have a beer, it was one of the few days we were allowed to relax.'

We talk some more about those days and he asked me about Frank's brother-in-law Jack Stancliffe .

'Now he was a character,' and we both laugh. 'Larger than life?' 'What, oh aye! Some of us lads went to see your Dad's home debut at Leicester, we went in that big fucking double-decker stand behind the goal, and cheered him on. Oh aye we were the best of mates and I was right proud he did so well for Leicester.'

Graham left the Cobblers in February 1968 to join York City. He returned to manage them to the Fourth Division championship in 1986/87, and is at the time of writing still involved in football as head scout at Newcastle United.

Frank Large's Northampton Town record

	League		*FA Cup*		*League Cup*	
	Apps	*Gls*	*Apps*	*Gls*	*Apps*	*Gls*
1966/67	21	8	0	0	0	0
1967/68	16	7	0	0	4	2

Total (all competitions): 41 appearances, 17 goals

10

Leicester City

FOR the first time in six moves we didn't have to follow Frank as a deal was done between the two clubs that allowed us to stay in Northampton – no removal van, no new house and importantly for me, no new school. It also probably suited Mum, who was nine months pregnant with our David.

On signing Frank, Matt Gillies was quoted as saying, 'I don't think I've ever seen a player with greater energy. He is just the type of hustling, bustling player we require. We shall use him as a twin striker with Mike Stringfellow, and I am hoping that his style of play will take some of the strain off Mike.'

Having sold the calibre of players such as Derek Dougan, Gordon Banks and Frank McLintock, Gillies was under pressure and with the team just three points off the bottom spot, results needed to pick up.

Richie Norman, who played over 300 games for Leicester in a career spanning ten years, remembers Gillies as 'an old-fashioned gentleman manager who always sat up in the stand. That season he knew we were struggling after a poor run of results and I know he was feeling the pressure.'

Unfortunately for Frank his First Division debut, away to Manchester City, saw them crushed 6-0 with Neil Young and Francis Lee grabbing a brace each. The newspapers pointed the finger at a defence 'as brittle as bone china'. A young Peter Shilton was blamed for two mistakes that cost two goals, and the all-round shocking defensive work saw a call for 'general recriminations, when three out of six goals are conceded with eight defenders in the box'.

As for Frank, the report added, 'His big-hearted aggressive effort relieved the monotony, but he was forced to hang about in a pitifully unsupported role.' He did however score seven out of ten to be City's best player on the night in the local paper – small consolation.

Frank's home debut against Arsenal is recalled by lifetime Leicester fan Chris Hudswell, who was at the match as a 13-year-old with his father in a crowd of 28,148.

He recalls, 'What I and my late father remembered most was that Len Glover was also making his debut. He had just signed from Charlton for £80,000, a record fee for a winger. What struck me and my dad was that in the few minutes before kick-off, Glover was surrounded by half a dozen photographers taking snap shots and that none of them took a picture of Frank. We both felt a bit sorry for him at the time.'

They didn't feel sorry for long, as with only three minutes gone Frank scored from a Bobby Roberts free kick, with a curling header that crept inside the post at the Filbert Street end.

It was Frank who stole the headlines that day, not only for his goal but his 'all-round performance that at times caused the Arsenal defence to panic'. On a half-frozen pitch Leicester appeared to be grabbing both points, getting to 2-1 (John Radford scored Arsenal's equaliser) with a Sinclair penalty, only for Arsenal to snatch a draw when Johnston netted with just three minutes to go.

Despite some shaky defensive work, Leicester probably deserved to win, and Gillies declared himself happy with the result and his debutants.

Bobby Roberts, the club captain, remembers the impact that Frank made and recalls the team's faults: 'We were a good cup team, played nice football, but were too easily rumbled and we needed somebody who could stand up to that.'

Leicester's record in the 1960s certainly proves this, reaching three FA Cup finals and two League Cup finals (winning only the League Cup in 1964, a game Bobby was dropped for despite scoring in both legs of the semi-final).

Bobby says, 'Your Dad gave us something in the box. You could get to the last third, and you knew you had an option, the goalies and the centre-halves didn't like it.'

A 0-0 draw with Sheffield United at Bramall Lane, which Mike Stringfellow missed through injury, prompted local journalist Jimmy Martin to note, 'Without making excuses, Leicester would probably have won this game had Stringfellow been playing. The other half of the twin spearhead Frank Large was in fine form and this pair I think could have forced victory.

'He [Frank] has been a surprise packet, improves with every game and his display was a considerable talking point.

Possessing remarkable stamina he never ceased to harry the United defence, and at least two snap shots from difficult positions had Alan Hodgkinson worried.

'It is beginning to look as if Leicester rescued a player who deserved better things than the obscurity of the Third Division. He certainly was the most dangerous forward on the field.'

I ask Bobby Roberts if Leicester adopted a more direct approach to facilitate Frank's strengths and his reply, in his soft Scottish accent, is interesting: 'Don't get me wrong he wasn't just a hard man, you don't get to play as many games or be signed by so many managers unless you can play, and he could. Frank was one of those lads who had waited for the chance to play at the top level, and when he did he grabbed it with both hands. He fitted in perfectly and gave us another option.'

Frank was quoted years later in his local paper, *The Mayo News*, on his time at Leicester, 'I really improved as a player that season, it was playing with better players that helped. The big difference was the fitness and the quality. In the lower divisions, you might have three or four good players on a team, but in the First Division all of the players were of a high quality. You'd make a run and the ball would be there before you, the midfield players used to see things so quickly.'

A landmark victory against Spurs at White Hart Lane is the first game I can remember seeing. A midweek kick-off under lights on a cold December evening saw Leicester win 1-0, their first away victory in five attempts. Having travelled down with Frank, me and our kid were being looked after by our 14-year-old uncle Dermot. After the match, as arranged, we waited by the players' entrance, when a door opened and as the steam slowly escaped we saw Frank sitting by the door, a towel over his lap, smiling and laughing.

Quick as a flash our Richard, just four years old, bolted towards the door and I followed, dodging the steward in his white butcher's coat, and we entered the holy of holies, the changing room.

Expecting a hug and a kiss we scampered towards Frank, who dealt with the matter immediately: 'What the fuck are you doing here? Get out!' As we gaped open-mouthed, the steward and Dermot appeared to escort us back up the tunnel. Poor old Dermot didn't half get a bollocking when Frank eventually got out.

A 2-2 draw at home to Manchester United saw the Foxes undefeated in five games, and four of them were draws. However, in those days of two points for a win, it didn't really hurt you as much as it does today.

Leicester got to play West Ham home and away over Christmas 1967, and the home match on Saturday 30 December was shown on *Match of the Day*. I remember being allowed to stay up and watch the game in my replica kit (which was way too big!) and Bobby Charlton Special football boots!

The fact that Frank scored and that Leicester lost 4-2 is completely forgotten but 25 years later Peter Mantle (the owner of Delphi Lodge) bought his handyman Frank the video *The Best of Match of the Day 1960s, 1970s and 1980s*, which unbelievably shows the game and the goal.

Frank slides in from the inside-right position on his arse and crashes a shot into the top-right corner. David Coleman.

commentating, simply says, 'Large, Large you beauty!' The pitch looks like the top three inches are totally liquid, and at the time it had the unenviable reputation as the worst in the league (Derby County and their infamous Baseball Ground were a couple of years away from the top flight).

The Leicester faithful had already taken Frank to their hearts and Chris Hudswell remembers that year's Christmas song was 'Ring the bells for Frankie Large la, la, la, la, la, la, la, la, la' to the tune of the Christmas carol 'Deck the Halls'.

The result mirrored the score from the Boxing Day match at Upton Park where Frank scored but a Brian Dear hat-trick and a Trevor Brooking goal saw West Ham home. These goals were followed by two against Sunderland in an away win at Roker Park, and another in a 3-1 defeat of Wolves at home.

With the pitch part-frozen, Wolves manager Ronnie Allan was desperate to get the game called off. This was Derek Dougan's first return to Filbert Street since his departure at the end of the previous season and one reporter noted, 'He might have been expected to turn in something special, however had it not been his job to kick off, I could say he never got a touch of the ball all afternoon.'

Away wins at Fulham (1-0) in the league and Barrow (2-1) in the FA Cup saw Leicester not only consolidating their league position, but also through to the fourth round of the Cup.

Having scored six goals in 12 games, Frank was now making the headlines in the national press, and his reputation for scoring with all parts of his body was enhanced in his next game at home against Leeds. In a tough encounter,

Frank scored a classic which I have already described (see the chapter *Northampton Town I*) in a 2-2 draw.

The fourth round draw pitted Leicester against Man City, who had not only humiliated them three months earlier, but had also knocked them out of the Cup in the previous two seasons. In front of 51,009 fans at Maine Road (the biggest crowd Frank ever saw) a turgid 0-0 draw that Bobby Roberts summed up as 'muck!' produced a replay two days later at Filbert Street.

Chris Hudswell has bitter-sweet memories, 'It was a school night and my dad would not let me go as there was a big crowd expected. This was Frank's match and the game has been described a the greatest ever seen at the City and I missed it! I see friends today who went and they say it's the best game they ever saw, Frank was inspirational that night.'

A full house of just below 40,000 witnessed the Lee, Bell and Summerbee show that saw City 2-0 up after just 25 minutes and coasting, thanks to a Lee penalty and a well-taken goal by Summerbee. Bobby Roberts remembers that game well, 'We were sluggish and found ourselves behind, but then we had a purple patch and Frank absolutely terrified their keeper Mulhearn – oh, and the centre-half Heslop. It was a real cup tie, the ball went end to end, and was in the box all the time, they couldn't live with your Dad.'

In a 20-minute spell either side of half-time Leicester came back from two down to 4-2 go up. Geoff Farmer wrote, 'Frank Large became a human battering ram at the head of a team that kept hurtling frantically forward.'

Their first goal came from Rodney Fern, a teenager playing only his third game, who having being set up by

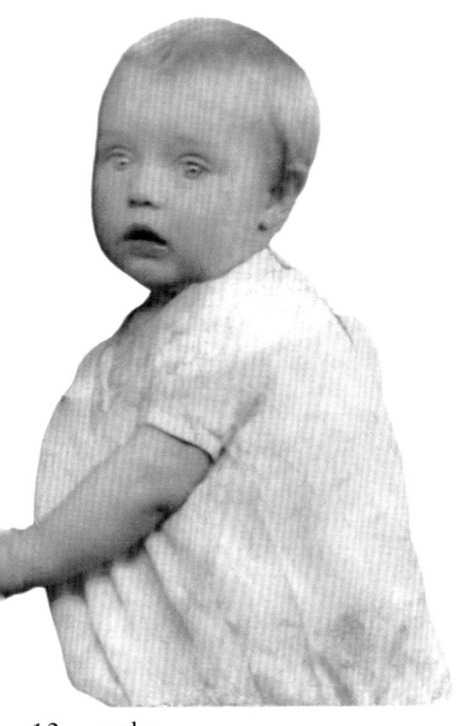

12 months.

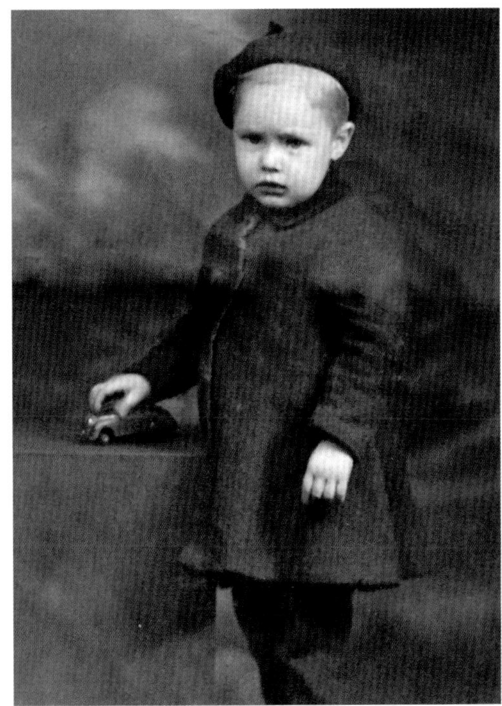

2 years.

Happy with his dogs.

NE SHILLING

★ Two teams on the cover every week

SOCCER STAR

HALIFAX 1961

coming in next week's edition:

● On the cover section of next week's edition are two more team group photographs, those of BLACKPOOL and BOURNEMOUTH. Stuart Shaw puts the focus spotlight on WOLVES, and Eric Batty again gives two pages of the latest news, tables and line-ups from overseas. Scotland and all Ireland will have their own exclusive sections as usual, and there will be two pages of English and Scottish after-match line-ups.

Halifax 1961.

Wedding Day,
7August 1961.

In full flow for QPR.

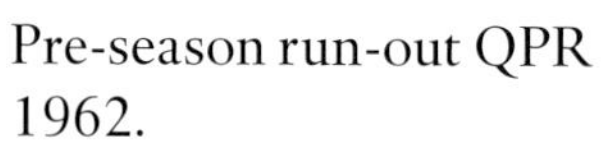

Pre-season run-out QPR
1962.

Northampton Town Division 3 Champions 1962/63.

"A typical day at the office", Carlisle. (Cumberland News)

Oldham 1966.
(Martin Smith)

Man with a suitcase, Oldham 1966, author far right.

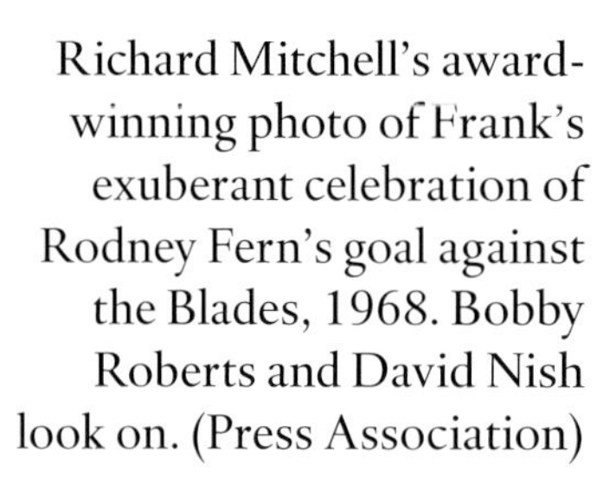

Richard Mitchell's award-winning photo of Frank's exuberant celebration of Rodney Fern's goal against the Blades, 1968. Bobby Roberts and David Nish look on. (Press Association)

Leicester 1967/68.
(Press Association)

Fulham 1968.
(Kenneth Coton)

Fulham, 1968.

Welcome to Fulham. (Kenneth Coton)

Robson, Large and Cohen. (Kenneth Coton)

Northampton Town 1971/72. Frank middle, front row.

Football's happy wanderer.

Frank Large with the ball…
USA 1974.

1974, next stop USA!
(Chronicle and Echo)

Mayo County Cricket Club 2000, Frank back left, author middle. (Ken Wright)

Cobblers reunion late 90s. (Peter Norton)

Deanshanger Oxide Works.

Delphi Lodge.

Frank, lashed in a terrific left-footed volley to score his first senior goal.

Bob Driscoll noted, 'Right from the start of the second half, the excitement in the packed Filbert Street ground zoomed as if Leicester's transformation had affected everyone. Five minutes later the atmosphere went up like a rocket, as big-hearted Large dashed on to another Fern shot to equalise.'

Ten minutes later Leicester were leading when a young David Nish headed home a Gibson cross to put City 3-2 up. Frank scored the fourth from a Nish corner, as 'he rose magnificently to nod in a beautiful fourth goal'.

Driscoll concluded, 'In a team of 11 heroes, two-goal Large deserved this garland. Even in those bleak opening minutes when Leicester were trailing he tirelessly sought to rally the attack.'

Colin Bell pulled back a third for City in the 87th minute, but Leicester survived to meet Rotherham in the next round. City had to be content with, eventually, the league championship and their great manager Joe Mercer was the first to congratulate the Leicester team, saying, Well lads, you thoroughly deserve what you fought for tonight. You should be proud of yourselves. Of course I am disappointed, when we were two goals up I thought we were in the next round, but Leicester never stopped running – and to put it briefly they ran my lads off their feet.'

Bert Johnson, acting manager due to Matt Gillies's illness, said, bursting with pride, 'I have seen some great performances by Leicester City over the years, but this one tonight must go down as one of the greatest.' Bobby Roberts certainly remembered it that way, and it has subsequently been voted as one of the best games ever at the old Filbert Street ground.

This euphoric victory only temporarily ended the hoodoo that the Manchester side had over the Foxes in the Cup but it did lead to a plethora of stories hailing Leicester's bargain buy of the century.

One read, 'Cheered on by the cries of the Filbert Street faithful, "Give us a goal, give us a goal Frankie Large" [he] must now be valued at £70,000.' Another said, 'Non-stop Large leaps into the £80,000 bracket as the buccaneering Third Division nobody has hit the First Division scene like a force ten gale.'

Bert Johnson's verdict on Frank was acutely prosaic, 'We needed a vigorous player, a chaser of lost causes. We knew we wouldn't be getting all these silky touches but what we were getting was a combative player who could use his weight in the front, and his height in the air. We were buying the heart of the man and that is the sort of thing you just cannot buy with money.'

Matt Gillies called him 'Mr Perpetual Motion', and this opinion was backed up by Richie Norman, who remembers, 'Frank was non-stop even in training. I remember we were playing forwards vs defenders and your Dad never stopped, he ran us ragged, and I said to him, "Bloody hell will you slow down"!'

A routine 3-1 away defeat at Anfield was followed by a 3-1 victory over Sheffield United at Filbert Street. Not only did Frank score his tenth goal in 17 matches in this match, but it also resulted in one of the best photos I have of him.

Celebrating Rodney Fern's goal, Frank is pictured with Fern folded over his right shoulder, in a fireman's lift, mouth open screaming in exhilaration as Bobby Roberts offers a quiet congratulatory pat, and David Nish arrives with a massive grin and a 'high five'.

The away FA Cup fifth round trip to Rotherham, then managed by Tommy Docherty, was no walkover, and Bert Johnson knew this as the Second Division outfit had already disposed of both Wolves and Aston Villa.

After watching a midweek friendly against continental opposition Inter Bratislava, Johnson took the trouble of walking on the deserted Millmoor pitch to assess the famous slope and the affect it might have on the game. Also the fact that Docherty's Chelsea had beaten Leicester in the 1965 League Cup Final rankled with the bosses.

A 1-1 draw was secured after Frank was brought down in the box by 17-year-old David Bentley. Regular penalty-taker Nish was foiled at his first attempt, but fortunately for Leicester, the linesman ruled that goalkeeper Mackleworth had moved. After lengthy protests from the home team, Nish hit the target and a replay was agreed for the following Wednesday.

In a fiercely competitive game, Frank broke his nose just before half-time but refused to come off because he saw that Peter Rodrigues was in a worse state and only one substitute was allowed in those days. As reported by Bob Driscoll, 'At one stage tempers flared when Large challenged the goalkeeper. Bentley rushed to his keeper's aid and then Large felled him with a left hook. Though it happened right in front of the referee the big Leicester man got away with it.'

Despite going close on a number of occasions Leicester failed to break down 'Docherty's locust storm of players' in normal time. It was only after three hours and one minute of intense dogged battling that Leicester seized the advantage.

Gibson swung in a corner and, according to a press report, 'The blonde head of Large towered above the red-shirted defenders of Rotherham to pound the ball into the net.'

Mike Stringfellow added another to see off the valiant challenge of 'Docherty's Dynamos', opening the way to a quarter-final berth against Everton.

The next day, as reported by Alan Williams in the *Daily Express*, 'Large strolled in to Filbert Street with a broken nose, double vision, a black eye, stitches in an eyebrow cut, a damaged shoulder and bruised and battered legs. He told acting boss Bert Johnson, "I'll be OK for Saturday's match at Chelsea. Don't worry."'

I ask Bobby Roberts if he could remember this. He said he couldn't but he wittily replied, 'He got that often, sometimes even in training!'

Bobby also sums up a part of what made Frank a success at that level: 'In those days the keepers came and punched the ball, and the forwards jumped with them. The amounts of clouts your Dad got in the face was amazing. He just got up and got on with it. He was absolutely fearless and when that ball went into the box, the keepers and the defenders knew it. They were totally aware of it, and often as a result it led to mistakes and chances.

'As I said your Dad gave us another option in the box, he was terrific because as a player if you couldn't go one way or the other you knew that if you put it in the mixer he could make something happen.'

I enjoy talking to Bobby. He sounds much younger than he is and you can feel a love for the game and a respect for Frank in the way he tells his stories with a mixture of pride and affection – I suppose the very qualities that made him a great club captain.

Not surprisingly Frank played three days later though Leicester were beaten 4-1 at Chelsea. Leicester's form in the run-in was very erratic, and despite playing in all of the 12 games, Frank failed to find the net.

Michael Parkinson, writing in *The Sunday Times* on the game against Arsenal, highlighted the fact that he felt Leicester were in danger of finishing the season the same way they started it. 'The defence even against an attack as prosaic as Arsenal's, was terribly vulnerable, the attack non-existent, except for Large's honest endeavour.'

Having avoided the real danger of relegation the team appeared to be happy for some mid-table mediocrity, and of course they had an FA Cup encounter to look forward to.

The quarter-final of the Cup was a first for Frank but not for Leicester who had an impressive record of achievement in the venerable competition during the 1960s. Another full house paid record receipts of £13,000 to see who would get through to the semi-final.

Despite being fancied by the local press, Leicester struggled to cope with a persistent Joe Royle who pushed and pulled the Leicester back four all over the pitch. While Frank tested Gordon West with a firm header from a Rodney

Fern cross, Jimmy Husband was beginning to wrest control of the midfield and constantly threatened Shilton's goal.

It was noted that Frank was in the thick of all things and constantly beat future England centre-half Labone in the air.

However it was Husband on 33 minutes who got the first goal but Nish equalised just before half-time, stabbing in a Gibson corner.

Leicester set up camp in the Everton half after the break but failed to convert any of the chances they made, and as often happens it was the opposition who broke away to score. Alan Ball worked in Howard Kendall, who volleyed in a Hurst cross. Leicester pushed again and Nish hit the bar, but had no luck and Frank's hard work got no reward as Everton sealed the game when Husband scored his second on 75 minutes.

Everton went on to the final where they lost 1-0 to West Bromwich Albion. It was the closest Frank ever got to a final. As for his team-mates they only had to wait for another 12 months.

As the season ended the prospect of a three-week tour to Zambia was initially seen as a bonus but the news that Fulham's young striker Allan Clarke had asked for a transfer from the relegated Cottagers started to grab the headlines.

Matt Gillies, back from his illness, took an interest, and much to Sir Matt Busby's annoyance agreed to take Clarke with Frank going to London. When I ask Bobby Roberts about the sale, he simply says, 'Matt used to make strange decisions – maybe to mix things up a bit.'

Richie Norman felt that Matt was planning a complete rebuild (he also left that summer) and, 'Clarke was not only younger than your Dad but also more cultured and I feel that Matt was looking to build a new team around him.'

Whatever the reason it certainly shook up not only Frank, but eventually all of us.

Pushed by the management and the chairman not to go to Zambia, but to stay and negotiate terms with the Fulham manager Bobby Robson, Frank refused and insisted on going to Africa. However under severe pressure he relented and agreed to sign for Fulham, after the trip to Zambia.

Frank told me it was the hardest decision he ever had to make as he believed that he had proven that he could perform at the highest level, and was desperate to stay there. Sadly Matt Gillies didn't and feeling unwanted he reluctantly agreed to the move. Apparently Bert Johnson was against the sale. If only his opinion had been taken on board.

The tour to copper-rich Zambia saw not only a 'motor coach from Filbert Street to London Heathrow Airport' but six matches including four against the Zambian International XI (FAZ XI).

The first game against the FAZ XI saw Leicester take 30 minutes to break the deadlock, before going on to win 6-1 with Frank grabbing an unusual headed hat-trick. *The Times of Zambia* reported, 'The FAZ XI played magnificent football for the first five minutes, almost overwhelming Leicester with sheer pace.' The home team's goal was scored by the intriguingly named Ginger Pencil.

Frank's final game for Leicester, in Lusaka against the national team, ended with a full-scale riot that saw the police using tear gas to hold back a disgruntled crowd who not only smashed windows, and attempted to set fire to the stadium, but also, more worryingly attempted to attack the Leicester team as they left the pitch.

Frank's version, quoted in the local press, nonchalantly stated, 'After the game we went up to get some tankards, we had won 3-2, but instead of a presentation all hell broke loose. The crowd threw bottles at us and didn't seem to mind whether they hit our players or their own. It was impossible to reach the dressing rooms, so the police got the tear gas out. They didn't seem to mind me too much – maybe because I scored – but I strolled around them and got into the room OK. I had to wait an hour before the rest of the lads got in!'

Scary enough, and knowing Frank he rarely made a drama out of things, but when you hear Bobby Roberts's account you have to wonder.

'Their goalkeeper was a local hero, and like most of the team played in bare feet. Anyway he comes for a cross and absolutely clouts Frank. Deliberately done and remember this is meant to be a friendly. Your Dad is badly hurt and the trainer wants to take him off, but he was not having that. He hobbles up and tells us all that at the first chance you've to put the ball up so I can hit him.'

I am spellbound as Bobby continues, 'Sure enough the ball is delivered and your dad absolutely carted him, and of course the keeper is stretchered off looking like he's dead! At the end of the match we attempt to get our trophies, but the riot kicks off and we have to run to the dressing rooms.'

Was it scary? 'Well there were quite a lot of police there with guns and gas and that, but we were held in the dressing rooms for over an hour while the windows were broken and there was lots of chanting outside…'

He drifts off and fails to answer the question. I prompt. Not too much to worry about then?

He starts laughing. 'I reckon it was your Dad they wanted [slightly different to his version!] and we had a toss-up about whether we should send Fulham's new centre-forward to meet the mob!'

Laughing, I thank Bobby for saving his life. Talk about going out with a bang. His last game for Leicester results in not only a goal, but a full-scale riot.

I thank Bobby for his time and for taking the trouble of getting back to me, and he stops me in my tracks. 'I know with Frank, wherever you go, whenever his name is mentioned, I've never ever heard anybody say a bad word about him.'

Honest? 'Aye it's unbelievable, I've never heard anyone say they didn't like Frank Large.'

Mischievously, I cannot resist saying, 'Johnny Haynes?' Bobby didn't miss a beat, 'Well remember this, Johnny Haynes didn't like anybody, he used to slag his own team-mates off all the time!'

I thank Bobby profusely for getting back to me and spending his time with me. Kindly he says, 'I hope the book goes well, your Dad thoroughly deserves it.'

What an absolute gentleman.

Frank Large's Leicester City record

	League		*FA Cup*		*League Cup*	
	Apps	*Gls*	*Apps*	*Gls*	*Apps*	*Gls*
1967/68	26	8	6	3	0	0

Total (all competitions): 32 appearances, 11 goals

11

Fulham

I HATED Allan Clarke! I can't exactly remember when it started, but the 1969 FA Cup Final saw my feelings reach their zenith. Watching from our lovely house in Chessington, as Clarke warmed up on the hallowed turf in an impossibly beautiful, technicolour blue shirt, with the fox's head proudly emblazoned on the badge, I realised that he was wearing Frank's shirt and that he should be out there getting ready to meet the minor Royal deputising for the Queen. Clarke's demeanour didn't help. Lank-haired, sulky and obviously under-fed, I couldn't understand how he could be better than my Dad!

I did know that as a result of Clarke moving to Leicester, I had had to leave Kingsley Park Primary where I had settled in well and loved my cap and blazer, and Hazeldine Road (although I'm sure our next-door neighbours Betty and Alan were pleased to see the back of me and our kid!) and my friends.

Frank had also left the top flight, never to return, and had just spent an unhappy year in and out of a struggling Fulham side that suffered relegation. My consolation was that Clarke had failed to keep Leicester up and was not going to lift the Cup. Spiteful for a six-year-old!

Twelve months later, the same lank-haired, cuff-clutching, skinny individual was lined up again at Wembley, this time in the white of Leeds United and while not my hero, he was cheered, along with the rest of the lads, as we attempted to win our first FA Cup. Frank, meanwhile, was back at Northampton in the Fourth Division.

December 1981

A cold, foggy morning on the training pitch behind the main stand at Elland Road (lovingly recreated in the film *The Damned United*). I am playing for Leeds University's first XI against a Leeds United A team and Frank, who is up in Leeds visiting family, is the only spectator as we run out in our hideous university colours – green shirts, green shorts and green socks.

The game is an annual fixture – professional clubs used to enjoy friendlies with us and later that season a young Norman Whiteside gets a run out at our university pitch in Weetwood as Man Utd travel over the Pennines – as new talent is blooded, debuted or assessed against 'sportsmanlike' opposition.

With no coach or manager our team talk is over quickly and as for the warm-up, it's every man for himself. This morning the list of future internationals includes David Seaman in goal, Denis Irwin at left-back and John Sheridan in midfield. Future Leeds stars Scott Sellars and Neil Aspin are also involved. These lads are playing to impress the numerous coaching staff who are huddled near the changing rooms, clip-charts in hand. Frank has the far touchline to himself.

For us it's a prestigious fixture, a chance to rub shoulders with the lucky few who have made it to a professional club, and possibly an opportunity to be plucked from obscurity.

As always it starts as an open and entertaining game (university football was renowned for this, and it's why we get the matches). However the mood is about to change.

Playing at centre-forward I win the first header against Aspin and despite a tough physical challenge do the same as the next long ball is delivered. Aspin gives me some verbals, which I ignore, barely understanding the thick Geordie accent.

Undeterred and enjoying the conflict, I climb for the next ball and miss it, falling to the ground clutching the back of my head, which feels like it's been hit with a hammer. Aspin is on top of me making sure I understand what he's done, spitting the words into my face. Ignoring the ball, he has head-butted the back of my head as hard as possible. An old trick!

Still seeing stars, I turn and tell him politely where to go. Game on. Toes are trodden on, testicles are grabbed, knees and elbows freely used.

I don't need to look at Frank to seek his approval, it's what he would do and I relish the challenge. As the game progresses and we take a lead, matching them in every department, the challenges get tougher and nastier. An end-of-term friendly becomes a battle royal.

Individual skirmishes erupt all over the pitch and the referee has to work hard to keep order. Ken Gibson (son of Scunthorpe United legend Archie), our normally genial left-back, has to be separated from a number of confrontations – most unlike him to be strangling a future pro footballer.

At 1-3 Leeds bring on the Scottish international Kenny Burns, who is coming back from injury, and thankfully for me he goes up front. As the match enters the last 20 minutes I notice that the Leeds manager Allan Clarke has entered the ground and is slowly walking around the pitch. As Clarke approaches Frank I watch intently to see if there is any contact at all between them.

Nothing, not a nod of the head or even a smile, let alone a handshake and an apology for stealing his First Division career. He keeps on walking and Frank keeps on watching.

With the clock running down we get a corner and the ball is whipped in, as Clarke stands by the post. I get across Aspin with the use of a well-sharpened elbow and head the ball past Seaman and into the net.

As I get up I catch Clarke's eye and smile broadly, (no response, just the frown he had worn all season, possibly all his life!), before jogging back to our half of the pitch.

The full-time whistle is blown and we have won 5-6. As we congratulate each other, the look on the faces of the Leeds lads says it all, 'beaten by a bunch of fucking students'. Bollockings are on the cards and contracts may be in jeopardy.

As I leave the pitch, happy with my overall performance and especially pleased with my goal, one of the Leeds coaches walks up, looks directly at me and smiles. Deep breaths, this might be a chance to make the grade. I wipe my hand and get ready to introduce myself, but sadly he walks past me and starts chatting to our Scouse midfielder (who'd had a blinder) and I realise, once again, that I'm not good enough.

A quick bath, the very same used by Charles, Charlton, Bremner et al, and I meet Frank in the car park. This is his own patch, he was born around the corner and had played against all those legends, his only regret being that he didn't get to play with them. A gentle pat on the shoulder is enough to let me know I did OK, no words are needed and we head off for a pint.

With hindsight I suppose I have to let Clarke off the hook. As a young goalscorer with great potential why would he choose to stay with a relegated team if there was the possibility of getting back into the top flight? There was a lot of interest and it looked a formality that he was going to Old Trafford, that's what Sir Matt Busby thought anyway. Bobby Robson was looking to get the best deal for Fulham and upset Sir Matt by rejecting his cash only offer of £150,000 in favour of Leicester's £120,000 plus Frank valued at £40,000.

What was Matt Gillies doing? Frank's goals had saved the Foxes from relegation and then a mid-table team broke the transfer record to sign the country's most sought-after young player. Bert Johnson, Gillies's assistant, was adamant that Frank should stay, but the decision was made and we were on our way to London and Clarke was off to Filbert Street.

Bobby Roberts told me, 'Matt had a habit of making strange decisions.' The previous season he had sold Gordon Banks and Derek Dougan for £50,000 each and he was soon to splash out £80,000 on Andy Lochhead.

Things initially appeared to go well at Fulham. Being wined and dined by the club was a first (and also a last!). A plush apartment was arranged while houses were scouted.

On Edgware Road near to Marble Arch, the building had a swimming pool and an underground car park.

Frank was paid a five per cent cut of his transfer fee, a cool £2,000, and was on a flat rate of £45 per week (plus bonuses). He also acquired a Brabham HB SL90 Viva, a beautiful car with black go-faster stripes over the bonnet that went round to the doors, plus twin carbs, an anti-roll bar and a modified exhaust. Jack Brabham had a garage and Frank got some off-season work there, and often popped home in exotic vehicles.

He appeared on the cover of Fulham's official handbook for 1968, doing a scissor-kick. Inside, Bobby Robson discussed the sale of Allan Clarke, saying, 'Now any fool can sell a good player for a high fee when there is such a demand. My job was to judge on the best offer, and believe me there were many astounding offers, some of them not reaching the ears of the press.

'Time will tell if I was right in accepting Leicester's bid. But I am sure I made no mistake. Money alone was no good to me because there are so few good players to be had. So I went for a player-exchange and of all the players offered Frank Large was my choice.

'I firmly believe that my faith in this experienced, enthusiastic forward will be rewarded. He has an infectious zest for the game and his new colleagues will respond to him – so will you. I wasn't proud to have sold Clarke, but I am happy to have the eager style of Frank Large on my side.'

How wrong could he be. Robson was sacked, Frank frozen out by Johnny Haynes and his cronies and booed by his own fans.

At the pre-season photo-call it was smiles all round and Frank was photographed next to World Cup winner and new team-mate George Cohen by Johnny Haynes, hamming it up for the London press. Danny Blanchflower, writing in his weekly column for the *Daily Express*, reflected the positive mood at Craven Cottage. He reckoned that relegation was not a bad thing and admonished Robson for feeling any guilt for allowing it to happen. The fact that Fulham had been struggling in the top flight for years, regularly escaping relegation at the last minute, was noted.

He continued, 'On the surface at least, Fulham seem to have got the better of the Clarke transfer deal. Allan Clarke is a talented young player who can get goals, but he is yet to prove himself a great player, one of outstanding merit. Perhaps Matt Gillies the Leicester manager sees him capable of that.

'Frank Large's enthusiasm helped Leicester a lot, he got vital goals for them, yet City did not have a very impressive season. They had to do something more. It would probably have suited them better to keep Large as well as buying Clarke, but Fulham wanted Large in part-exchange.

'Large's enthusiasm could do a lot for Fulham. He might not get as many goals as Clarke but his effort could have a more telling effect for the team. And with £110,000 to spend on other players as well Robson is in a position to give Fulham the better end of the deal.'

Blanchflower also examined the role of Haynes, beginning his 19th season at Fulham, and posed the question that maybe they should be looking to plan without the great man as they aspire to return to the top division.

So with everything looking rosy, a black and white Fulham duffel bag became my new prized possession (my beloved Leicester shirt relegated, albeit temporarily). With no school or garden the corridor of the apartment becomes our football pitch, and despite complaints from the neighbours and frequent visits to the nearby Hyde Park, our favourite pitch measures ten yards by two yards.

A defeat in a friendly, a game Frank missed through injury, led the *Soccer Star* to report, 'On the evidence of Fulham's friendly at Southend last Saturday, their main hopes of a quick return to the First Division will rest on Frank Large.'

Despite the omens, they began the campaign with a 1-0 win over Bristol City quickly followed by a 1-1 draw at Aston Villa. This however was followed by a shocking run of six games in which they failed to score a goal, drawing two and losing four on the trot.

A desperate Robson looked to pep up the forward line and introduced an untried youngster, Malcolm Macdonald. Frank told me that Macdonald's talents and abilities were discussed at a team meeting and he said that he reckoned he was a natural and that he should be given a chance. He recalls that Haynes and a few of his clique laughed at the suggestion, but Robson took it in and sure enough Macdonald made his debut away at Oxford United in a 1-0 defeat.

After 540 minutes without scoring, Fulham, with Macdonald and Frank up top together, took the field against Crystal Palace. It was Frank's 400th competitive game and as they walked out of the tunnel Macdonald turned to Frank and asked, 'What's the plan Frank?'

'If you see the onion bag, give the ball a good leather!' came Frank's succinct reply. It obviously worked as Macdonald scored in a 1-0 win.

The home game against Blackburn has been preserved for posterity on YouTube and the video shows Frank at his barnstorming best. He terrorises the goalkeeper and centre-halves, throwing himself into every challenge, and is unlucky not to score.

A typical opportunist chase sets up Fulham's goal. Dispossessing the right-back, he races towards the left edge of the 18-yard box and cleverly flicks the ball with his left heel, shifting it on to his right foot before cutting it back for Haynes, on the edge of the box.

Haynes attempts to pass the ball into the bottom-left of the goal, but Macdonald intercepts it and smashes it into the other corner. Haynes was not happy with the goal and moaned that his shot was going in and that Macdonald should not have intervened. The footage shows that was not going to be the case. Macdonald was not best pleased.

Frank finally got on the scoresheet with a brace in the next game, a 5-4 defeat at Birmingham for whom Jimmy Greenhoff scored four. However, the poor run of results led to Robson's sacking. He wistfully recalled in his autobiography that the club was regrouping and in a comfortable eighth position in the league. The unfortunate reality was that by mid-November they were just outside the relegation zone.

Unbelievably Frank could at this stage have been back in the top flight, ironically at Leicester. John Hutchinson, the Foxes club historian, showed me the minutes from the directors' meeting of 28 October 1968:

'The manager then reported on the availability of players in whom he had an interest, and that a discussion had taken place with the Fulham Football Club regarding the possibility of obtaining the transfer of Frank Large for a fee somewhere in the region of £20,000.'

We don't know what Fulham's response was. As for Frank, I know he wasn't consulted and I also know that until his dying day he never knew that Leicester had made an official approach!! (Fulham, however, eventually sold him ten months later for £12,000.)

Along with Bobby's departure Frank was dropped and made his first career appearance as a substitute in a game against Charlton. Johnny Haynes was appointed player-manager, and while George Cohen later suggested that he was reluctant to take the job, Robson drily noted that, 'Johnny lasted 28 days at a club where he was a legend. He was a great guy and an illustrious player, but he was never manager material.'

Malcolm Macdonald felt that Robson was undermined by the senior players, Haynes being the main instigator. Cohen acknowledges that Robson felt he didn't get enough support, but fails to go into detail.

Frank is famously quoted as saying, 'The only man I was ever scared of on a football pitch was Johnny Haynes.' This about his team-mate, captain and erstwhile manager. Frank explained this to me. He told me that Haynes would sometimes deliberately set out to make you look a bad player, like not moving for a pass 'unless it was on his big toe, he could destroy your confidence' and with the team struggling and a new young manager it was a lethal combination.

Macdonald wrote in his autobiography *Never Afraid to Miss*, 'I can't help feeling sorry for Haynes. He was Mr Fulham and he loved the club and people. It must have destroyed him to feel his career ending and to watch a new generation of players coming into the club to take over his team. I can't forgive him for the way he treated us, but now strangely, I understand. It was almost a form of jealously as he reluctantly let his association slip.'

I know Frank felt the same way and while he enjoyed his company off the pitch, he grew to hate him on it.

So I suppose that Johnny Haynes was the villain of the piece. Frank had a manager who believed in him (one who would go on to succeed at the highest level) and a team reckoned to be capable of mounting a promotion push, we got a lovely house and the car, even the new school I went to was OK but not a patch on Kingsley Park. What a crying shame, it should have been so different.

By the time Bill Dodgin was brought in as manager, Frank was being utilised as a makeshift centre-half, a position he hated. An impressive debut at number five came in the third round of the FA Cup away to top-flight Sunderland in a 4-1 win. The next round brought the holders West Bromwich Albion to the Cottage and an exit from the esteemed competition as the Baggies won 2-1.

A number of appearances as a sub ended a horrid year. A start in the final game in front of 36,521 at Selhurst Park saw Palace secure a historic promotion to the First Division and Fulham relegated to the Third Division, although Frank scored his third and last goal for the club.

He couldn't wait to get away. At first it looked likely that Tommy Docherty was going to take him to Villa, then it was Alec Stock, Frank's former boss at QPR, who wanted to re-unite him with Macdonald, who had left at the end of the season, at Luton.

Instead it was Dave Bowen who stepped in to buy him for a third time. Frank was never so pleased to be leaving a club, and of course to be returning to one he knew so well, albeit by now in the bottom tier of the Football League.

Frank Large's Fulham record

	League		*FA Cup*		*League Cup*	
	Apps	*Gls*	*Apps*	*Gls*	*Apps*	*Gls*
1968/69	19(4)	3	2	0	1	0
1969/70	1	0	0	0	1	0

Total (all competitions): 24(4) appearances, 3 goals

12

Northampton III

THINGS had not gone well for the Cobblers in the two seasons since Frank had left for the top division. Tony Marchi failed to have his contract renewed and he was replaced by the former England international Ron Flowers, who was promoted from player-coach to player-manager. Unfortunately his only season in charge saw them relegated to the Fourth Division. This made them the first team ever to climb from the bottom tier to the top and go back again, all achieved in a decade.

Dave Bowen had returned as manager and immediately set about rescuing Frank from his Fulham nightmare. Upon signing, Frank was interviewed by the *Chronicle and Echo*. Asked to explain his many moves he stated, 'Whenever my manager has told me another club want me, and it has been left up to me, I have felt sort of unwanted, so I have mainly accepted the move and off we have gone. I've never been the sort of fellow who argues terms either, but football has given me a great living and I'm grateful anyway.'

As for being snatched by the Cobblers again, and Dave Bowen in particular, he added, 'It really was like coming home at last, it felt great, my family did too and we moved into a new house in Northampton within a fortnight of signing. We just couldn't wait to get there.'

The new house was detached, just off Acre Lane, 1 Harvest Way (built by local firm Wilcon) and was to be ours for an unprecedented two-and-a-bit years.

Most poignantly, Frank reckoned that, over his 11-year career so far, 'I have been jeered in the south, cheered in the north and loved in the Midlands.'

Bowen had now signed Frank three times for the same club in the same decade – a record I don't reckon will ever be repeated. Frank was also the first player to join the club for a third stint since the legendary Herbert Chapman in 1907.

His debut was in a comprehensive 4-1 defeat at Port Vale, Graham Felton scoring the consolation goal. Graham was a fair-haired winger who notched up 254 league games for the Cobblers in a ten-year spell at the club. I bumped into him at the new Sixfields Stadium, instantly recognising him with time having been very kind to him.

Introductions over, I asked him what it was like to play with Frank? 'A dream for a winger, all you had to do was put it into the box and your Dad would make something of it. He always caused trouble in the penalty box, never stopped running and boy could he head a ball.'

The Cobblers' form that season was erratic and they had to wait seven games before their first win (4-1 over Newport County, Frank scoring two). This was followed by wins over Notts County (3-1) and Bradford Park Avenue (2-1) with Frank scoring in both matches.

Bradford were captained that day by Frank's old mate Graham Carr.

September 1969 was significant for an incident at Swansea City where Frank was sent off for only the second time in his professional career. Swansea had galloped into a 3-0 lead, but the Cobblers wouldn't lie down and made a spirited comeback, with goals by Neil Townsend and the Swansea-born 17-year-old Peter Hawkins.

As Northampton pressed for an equaliser Frank had a fierce shot miss the target and hit a young boy behind the goal. As he approached to see if the lad was OK, two Swansea supporters jumped from the crowd and started attacking him. Naturally Frank defended himself and when the fracas was broken up he was duly sent off by the referee. To make matters worse Hawkins was also subsequently sent off and not surprisingly they failed to draw level.

The club appealed the decision and the FA Disciplinary Committee meeting in the Midland Hotel in Birmingham took just 25 minutes to clear Frank of the charge. The verdict was, 'The committee is satisfied that Large acted in self-defence and was not guilty of violent conduct. The committee have decided that no further action will be taken.'

A letter from one of the attackers, Bill Carroll, was read out at the hearing. Interestingly Carroll was a former professional footballer who had been on the books of Sheffield Wednesday and West Bromwich Albion, though he never made either first team.

He confessed that he had become overcome with emotion on seeing the child hurt, as he had lost his own son through illness. There is no account of any punishment he and his colleague received for their actions.

The rest of the season was up and down, one major consolation being an excellent FA Cup run, the other being the goalscoring partnership that developed between Frank and John Fairbrother. Frank's all-action style suited John who went on to score 23 league goals with Frank managing ten. John became the first Cobblers player to grab more than 20 in a season since Alec Ashworth in 1963. A mid-table finish of 14th at least saw the side consolidating, after the free-fall of the previous three seasons.

The FA Cup run started somewhat inauspiciously with a 0-0 draw with non-league Weymouth in the first round in November. A 3-1 win three days later at the Wessex Stadium in front of a record crowd of 4,500 saw them progress to the second round and a home tie against Exeter City.

With Northampton trailing 1-0 to Exeter, and with just three minutes to go, the future Liverpool full-back Phil Neal, who had come on as a substitute, grabbed an equaliser that rescued the Cobblers.

The replay resulted in a 0-0 draw though it was hardly boring as the Cobblers had three goals disallowed and Exeter one of their own. The third and deciding game in this drawn-out trilogy was played at the County Ground, Swindon, in squelching mud, and resulted in a 2-1 win for Northampton with Frank on target.

With the 'big boys' now in the hat, a taxing away trip to non-league Brentwood was not the best draw. One small consolation was that Brentwood's chairman was the England legend Jimmy Greaves.

The match was postponed twice, once because of the weather and the second time as a result of a flu epidemic. Eventually the game was played on 10 January and a bumper crowd of 5,320 packed into the little ground to see the Cobblers progress through a solitary John Fairbrother goal.

Tranmere away was the reward. A dour 0-0 draw on Merseyside, ruined by gale-force winds, led to game number eight in what was only the fourth round to be scheduled three days later.

As was the norm in those days the draw for the next round was conducted, without any fanfare, at noon on the following Monday and broadcast live on BBC Radio 2. I am sure both teams will have gathered around the wireless to hear the news that whoever won the replay would get to face Wilf McGuinness's Manchester United, at home.

As a result of this, the Cobblers pulled in 16,142 fans, their biggest gate for over three years. A headed assist by Frank allowed Graham Felton's deflected shot to give the Cobblers the lead on 20 minutes. Tranmere equalised in the 35th minute when the soon-to-be-famous Kim Book failed to hang on to a long throw, but the Cobblers restored their lead in the seventh minute of injury time through a Frank Rankmore header.

A nervy second half saw no more goals and was noticeable only for the complete lack of quality and an altercation that led to the referee, Keith Walker, threatening to abandon the match because somebody in the ground was using a whistle to disrupt play. The local paper, the *Chronicle and Echo*, wryly hinted that he would have done as good a job as the actual 'man in black'.

Now the build-up to the fifth round tie could begin. A comprehensive 3-0 victory over Bradford was watched by nearly 13,000, some 8,000 more than the average league attendance. This was because a voucher system was put in place, allowing attendees at this match entitlement to tickets for the United game.

Cup fever hit Northampton in a big way. The first to cash in was the club itself, upsetting many supporters by increasing ticket prices for this one-off game. A season ticket holder's seat went up from £1 10/ (£1.50) to £2, the Hotel End rose from 5/6 (27p) to 12/ (60p), while the Spion Kop doubled from 5/ (25p) to 10/ (50p). The match programme cost 2/.

Numerous incentives were offered to the players by local businesses and supporters alike, all geared towards free publicity in the run-up to the big day. Frank Grande (the present club historian) had the pleasure of fitting four new tyres – gratis – to Frank's turquoise Mini Clubman. The local paper engineered a photo shoot with Frank, John Fairbrother and Dixie McNeill pointing 12-inch shotguns at the camera, no doubt to be run under the old clichéd headline 'Gunning for success'. Flags and scarves adorned every shop and public building.

The club organised for an additional temporary stand to be erected alongside the existing temporary stand that flanked the cricket pitch. Then, as now, the County Ground was owned by Northamptonshire County Cricket Club. The outfield trespassed on to the football pitch in the summer and the temporary stand had to be removed – the rest of the pitch was used as a car park.

The idea was to cram in as many people as possible – including a percentage from Manchester. It worked and the official attendance was recorded as 21,771. This figure, however, was hotly disputed by the players who were paid bonuses on the size of the gate. I remember Frank had a healthy disdain for the official number, grumbling that it was often obviously thousands lower, enabling the club to cheat not just the players, but also the taxman.

Our kid and I's pre-match ritual that season had been to accompany Frank to the ground probably an hour before kick-off, wander in through the players' entrance, an innocuous door at the back of the main stand, and see Frank disappear into the changing rooms leaving us with the whole empty stadium to ourselves for what seemed like an eternity.

Having scampered all over the place we eventually took our seats in the main stand – well, wooden benches – below the directors' box, which was wooden benches with cushions!

We were absolutely desperate to stand in the Hotel End with the Cobblers fanatics, but as mentioned Mum made sure that we sat in the main stand with Yorkie, a Halifax lad in his early 60s who was living in Northampton, a dear family friend, and a 100 per cent wonderful man. Part of the attraction of the Hotel End was the fact that it was they who used to start the song 'He's here, he's there, he's every fucking where, Frankie Large'.

Particular spice was added to this game, which was just prior to the scourge of hooliganism that defined the 1970s and 1980s, when it was widely rumoured that some 'hards' from the Hotel End were gonna give the northerners a good kicking. Police reported no incidents of violence on the day.

Anyway with the players being treated to a pre-match steak dinner at the Westone Hotel, we had to rely upon uncle Yorkie to bring us to the match.

According to Frank, Dave Bowen's pre-match talk focussed on the importance of attempting to blot out the influence of midfield maestro Bobby Charlton. Georgie Best was barely discussed, having been suspended by United for a number of misdemeanours, and it seemed unlikely that he would be taking part – but unfortunately for the Cobblers he did.

If you type Northampton v Manchester United into YouTube you can get to watch extended highlights of the game, broadcast at the time by the local ITV franchise Anglia. The game was shown on the Sunday with no studio build-up, no ex-pros discussing tactics, and the coverage's opening credits cuts to the team sheets, imposed over the players as they wander on to the pitch.

The camera focusses on Frank who is swinging his arms vigorously (this, along with Mac, the trainer, digging his bionic thumbs into oiled thighs, constituted the warm-up). The commentator notes Frank's physical threat and as the match begins you notice that approximately 21,000 of the crowd are wearing khaki-green parkas – it is February after all.

The early exchanges are tentative and Northampton appear to be holding their own on a sticky surface that is already beginning to cut up.

But then a nothing cross is missed badly by Kim Book, the brother of Manchester City captain Tony, and Best nods home his first goal. It is soon 2-0 as Crerand brilliantly slots a precision pass, from inside his own half, into the path of Best, who coolly goes around the onrushing Book on the edge of the 18-yard box and strokes it home.

Book makes an outstanding save from Kidd, who volleys from seven yards, after Crerand, who is running the show, feeds Morgan to cross. A small scuffle is unfolding behind the goal (in front of the Hotel End) and Book's effort is missed by the photographers as they clamour to get a picture of the hooliganism. The police appear to deal with it quickly.

The Cobblers get in at half-time only two down and Frank has hardly seen the ball, let alone touched it.

Best then grabs his hat-trick, poking home from inside the box at the second attempt, his first effort desperately blocked on the line. A rare Cobblers attack results in McNeill being chopped down by Edwards in the box and a penalty is awarded. Rankmore, the Cobblers' captain, calmly clips it to Stepney's right, but the goalkeeper manages to touch it on to the post and then makes a brilliant instinctive stop as Fairbrother drills in the rebound.

Kidd chips in a cross from the left and Best, unmarked, ghosts in with a header to make it 4-0 before Book pulls off a fine save from Charlton but the subsequent corner finds Kidd unmarked in the six-yard box to net the fifth.

A long punt forward falls to Best and with Rankmore galloping to catch up, he guides the ball into Book's right-corner from the edge of the box for 6-0, and it is soon seven as from a rare Cobblers attack right-back Fairfax goes on an overlap, but Ross's poor cross is intercepted and the gaping hole at the back is exploited by Morgan, whose shot is parried to Kidd, who taps in his second.

At last the Cobblers get something back as a good ball from Ross puts Clarke in on the right and his deep cross is fumbled by Stepney, under pressure from Frank, and McNeill finds the back of the net.

Then a long ball from McNeill frees Frank who finds himself one on one with Stepney. He gets round the goalkeeper and under pressure from a defender he attempts to guide the ball in from a very tight angle on the left, but unfortunately it goes across the open goal.

United immediately counter-attack and as the Cobblers fail to clear their lines the ball falls to Best and with only Book to beat, he drops his right shoulder, forcing Book to dive. Best then taps it into the other side of the goal to make the score 8-1.

Looking rather sheepish he walks to the post, pauses and then begins to walk back up the pitch, no celebration and no recognition that he had just set a new team scoring record.

Fairbrother finds some space on the left and puts in a perfect cross that eludes Ure and Frank nods home inside Stepney's left post to complete the scoring at 8-2. As he turns to celebrate you notice how clean his shirt and shorts are, certainly compared to his colleagues at the back. It also looks like Mum had been trimming his hair.

Frank's goal prompts one local radio reporter to announce, 'Yes, Northampton are making a comeback!' As the final whistle is blown Best is stood by the tunnel and leaves the pitch instantly, followed quickly by the rest of the players, as the obligatory pitch invasion begins. Desperate to join in, we sit spellbound as thousands mill aimlessly on the muddy expanse, waiting for Yorkie to give us the nod.

Frank Grande recalls Dixie McNeill saying, 'Every now and again they show those goals on the TV. No doubt Frank [Large] like myself wonders why our goals aren't shown.'

In the fourth round in 2004, history repeated itself and Manchester United were drawn away to Northampton. Most of the build-up on Sky concerned the match 34 years earlier, and Frank and Dixie's goals were finally acknowledged, but sadly Frank had already passed away.

George Best (he died shortly after) was reunited with Kim Book at the now-defunct football pitch at the County Ground. The Cobblers were beaten 3-0 at their new home, Sixfields.

Interviewed in the *News of the World* in July 1999, Frank remembers 'The day Bestie sank me'. The headline caps a piece in which Frank is pictured in a rowing boat, on Doolough, Delphi, Connemara – nice to see the clichés don't improve with time. Talking about Best's performance he says, 'He tortured our full-backs that day. None of us could get close enough to kick him – and lord knows we tried. That was the only time I came off the pitch, knowing I had been up against an opponent who was better than I could ever be.' After the match Dave Bowen got all the Cobblers players to sign the ball, along with the words 'George you are the greatest', and it was presented to the six-goal hero. Kim Book said, 'The only time I got near George was to shake his hand at the end.' Best reckoned, 'After the match I saw their goalie, Kim, and nodded my head, and he dived into the gutter.'

Despite the bumper pay-day, club chairman Eric Northover controversially suggesting in the *Chronicle and*

Echo that he felt 'the Northampton team were disgraceful'. Outraged, the players demanded an apology, but were given the excuse that his words had been taken out of context.

One final footnote to that fateful day was my brother's recollection (on the Cobblers' website after the 2004 game) that he got his first kiss that Saturday, 7 February 1970, at the age of six, from Frank Rankmore's daughter! As I was ultimately responsible for him that day, I must apologise to Frank and his daughter – I however have no memory of this!

The rest of that season was anti-climactic and a mid-table finish deemed satisfactory, if a tad disappointing. The only highlight was England's upcoming defence of the World Cup, and the team song 'Back Home' being belted out with gusto by the County Ground faithful as the tournament approached.

That summer is fondly remembered. Our Esso World Cup coins had been collected, Terry Cooper proving extremely difficult to obtain in the greater Northampton area. A new colour TV was acquired, rented from Multi-Broadcast, and we all settled down to watch England retain the Jules Rimet Trophy.

Fascinated by the notion of aertex shirts, salt tablets and David Coleman's commentary, we immersed ourselves in everything Mexican and as we cruised towards a semi-final berth against Italy, I even decided to forgive Jeff Astle for his miss against Brazil in the group game.

Game over, me and our kid left the sitting room to go in the garden and re-enact the goals just as Bobby Charlton departed the pitch in Guadalajara. Suddenly we heard a pained shout, and ran back in to realise that Germany had pulled one back. Still no need to panic, we headed out again only to be disturbed by Frank swearing loudly at the TV. Concerned, we rushed in and realised the worst had happened. We sat glued to watch the next painstaking 30 minutes and saw 'The Cat' fail to deal with 'Der Bomber' and England were out and on their way home having been 2-0 up with 20 minutes to go.

We watched the final on a campsite in Dorset. Cobblers secretary Jimmy Andrews had a static mobile home just above Durdle Door, an idyllic location, and we had the most amazing time there. Pele joined Frank as my all-time favourite player as he led the greatest team in history to their third World Cup.

That summer I also got my first job, working as a butcher's delivery boy, with Mick, a mate of Frank's, travelling around Northamptonshire on Fridays, getting fed and paid 10/ (50p) and delivered home just in time for *Hawaii Five-O*. We also got a sister, Victoria, the third child born in Northampton.

As that great summer drew to a close Frank was interviewed by *Soccer Star*, along with Don Masson of Notts County, Nobby Lawton of Brighton & Hove Albion, and John Regan of Doncaster Rovers.

Looking forward to the new season Frank was asked who to tip for the top spot and he picked Notts County, who were the eventual champions, whereas Don tipped Aldershot – who ended up 14th.

As for their own team's chances, Frank reckoned top four, and Don felt that if Notts could 'tighten up at the back' they would do well. No doubt Bob Worthington helped enormously in that department.

As for potential newcomers, Frank mentioned a half-back called Phil Neal – who went on to win every honour possible with Liverpool and enjoyed a successful career with England.

Finally, discussing priorities, all cited promotion. Frank however could not resist saying, 'I'd like to think that we could play Manchester United again and this time beat them!'

Despite the cup run, the club actually lost money that season – £47,000. As a result Dave Bowen was restricted to making one signing, Keith East, a forward from Bournemouth.

The 1970/71 season started brightly with three consecutive wins, two of which were away from home, and undefeated after ten matches the Cobblers sat proudly at the top of the table. They also progressed in the League Cup with wins over Scunthorpe United, for whom Kevin Keegan scored a penalty, and York City after two replays, setting up a third round tie with Second Division side Aston Villa.

In front of 15,072 fans Villa took a 1-0 lead, but Frank equalised with a shot of such ferocity it nearly took the back off the net. Interviewed many years later in March 2001, in the Oldham Athletic match programme for a game against Northampton, Frank remembers that strike as one of his best goals: 'Northampton drew 1-1 at home to Aston Villa in the FA Cup [sic], and I hit one from outside the penalty area which flew into the top corner, and it gave me a lot of pleasure.'

Unfortunately Villa won the replay 3-0 and an early exit in the FA Cup to future giant-killers Hereford United left the Cobblers with just the league to focus on.

The *Football League Review* used a photo shoot of Frank parading his past teams' shirts in order on its front page, in the style of *Rowan & Martin's Laugh-In.* The shirts had kindly been provided by the clubs, but were not the ones that Frank actually wore. Halifax's and QPR's had round collars, while Northampton's 1963 shirt had morphed into a much later edition. The final picture showed a bare-chested Frank holding up two fists to indicate no clubs.

Inside, under a heading titled 'The Happy Wanderer', Frank was pictured with his current boss Dave Bowen, and was asked his opinion on his numerous moves. 'It's been great fun with great clubs, but I couldn't have done it without my wife. She has been wonderful, as moving from house to house produces so many problems...and it is difficult to keep real friends when you are always on the go.'

According to my calculations between 1962 and 1972, I lived in 13 different homes and attended five different primary schools.

Despite maintaining a promotion place all season fate was to deal a cruel hand. Club captain and stalwart centre-half Frank Rankmore picked up a career-ending injury away to Bournemouth at the end of January. The former Welsh international was sorely missed, not just at the back, but also his presence at set pieces, where his aerial ability often resulted in crucial goals.

The young Neil Townsend took over but as his inexperience began to show, Bowen looked to steady the ship with an older head. Frank's time at Fulham included several stints at centre-half but he genuinely disliked playing there. He told me once that as a forward you are generally focussed on the ball, which for a defender can prove to be disastrous. Regardless, he was given the stop-gap job and on his debut in the number five shirt he had a blinder in a 2-0 home win, that not only saw a first clean sheet in five games, but also a goal and a booking on a personal note.

Despite the tweaking they struggled to maintain any consistent form and the 5-0 demolition of Workington, with Frank back in attack, saw him score and get an injury that meant he missed the last three games of the season.

He didn't miss much, the Cobblers lamely going down to Barrow (who finished bottom and only had another season to go in the league before failing to be re-elected), Southport and Southend. After 46 games they missed out on promotion by just five points.

Elsewhere, a young Dave Worthington – Bob – won his first silverware as Notts County walked the league.

The 1971/72 season was widely considered a shocker for Northampton as they had to apply for re-election having finished 21st in the Fourth Division, for the first time in the club's history. Frank however had a great goalscoring run, bagging 19 league goals in his 44 appearances (the highlight being an 18-minute hat-trick against Chester), which included six starts at centre-half. Not a bad return for a 31-year-old in a struggling team.

Dave Bowen's failure to replace Rankmore led to Frank pulling on the number 5 shirt again, but by September somebody saw sense and Lew Chatterley was signed from Aston Villa. This allowed Frank to move back up front where he was badly needed as Fairbrother left for Mansfield, to be followed by McNeill who went to Lincoln.

Another FA Cup defeat to non-league Hereford and patchy form all season, which saw them fail to register a single victory in any of their last eight league games, led to their (fortunate) re-election.

Another player who had a good season, breaking into and then establishing himself in the first team, was John Buchanan. A 20-year-old Scot signed from Ross County, the attacking midfielder went on to play 193 games – scoring 36 goals, many with his explosive left foot – for the Cobblers in two spells.

I had the pleasure of playing with John in the early 1980s with non-league Wolverton Town. He was a lovely character, kind and helpful to a young lad trying to make his way in the game, and still a bloody good footballer. He also thought highly of Frank and they managed to meet over a pint after one home match and talk about the good old days.

John had a great sense of humour and having played in the European Cup Winners' Cup against the mighty Real Madrid, having qualified by winning the Welsh Cup with Cardiff, he kept us all laughing when confronted with changing rooms that had paraffin heaters, cold showers and no coat pegs by saying, 'Eh lads, it's no' quite the Bernabeu!'

The 1972/73 season saw Bowen rebuilding the side with experienced pros in the hope that he could once again get the team challenging for promotion. Former Ipswich Town captain Bill Baxter joined from Hull City, along with Doncaster Rovers centre-half Stuart Robinson and Dietmar Bruck, a wing-half from Charlton Athletic.

Another unimpressive start eventually resulted in Dave Bowen deciding to move upstairs, for the final time, to become general manager/secretary. Bill Baxter took over the day-to-day job as player-manager.

Dave Bowen remains one of the great unsung managers of all time. Apart from the 'miracle' of getting Northampton Town from the Fourth Division to the First Division, his loyalty saw him turn down the opportunity to manage Manchester City, Sunderland and his own national team, Wales, though he did manage them part-time for a while. While at Northampton, it was only the board who stopped him signing such young talent as Mike Summerbee, Colin Bell, Mike England and Francis Lee, who all progressed to glittering international careers. He did develop local talent with Phil Neal, John Gregory and George Reilly netting £250,000 for the club, however. Finally, of course, he signed Frank on three separate occasions, only selling him once, the pair having a great deal of mutual respect.

Baxter's first move as manager was to sanction the release of Frank, who was playing in the reserves, having been dropped as the goals dried up with none in eight starts.

As always he was giving 100 per cent, and Paul Stratford (who went on to become a prolific scorer for the club himself) remembers asking Frank for the day's tactics, as they stood over the ball, ready to kick off a reserve match.

'To put the ball in the back of the net as many times as possible!' came the answer. Frank Grande smiles as he says, 'Typical of your Dad. He once told me, "I can only do one thing, but I am good at it."'

Frank's last game for the Cobblers was on 16 November 1972 – a 2-0 FA Cup defeat to local rivals Peterborough United at London Road. Ironically one of Frank's team-mates that day was Dietmar Bruck, who had actually played against Frank when he had made his debut for the Cobblers on 2 March 1963.

Northampton finished that season in their lowest ever position, 23rd in the Fourth Division. Frank finished 16th in the Third Division having signed for Chesterfield where he scored nine goals in 23 games.

Bill Baxter's decision to let him go meant that Northampton had paid a total of £35,000 for Frank's services, recouping £38,000 in sales and benefitting from 96 goals in 248 appearances.

Frank is still fondly remembered at Sixfields, the new home of Northampton Town Football Club, and through the honest endeavours of Frank Grande (to name but one) the club present an annual 'Frank Large Supporter of the Year Award' to the person voted by the fans as the best supporter that season. The event takes place at the last home game of the season, on the pitch, just before kick-off, and as a family we try to attend. It is a lovely gesture from the club Frank held closest to his heart.

Frank Large's Northampton Town record

	League		*FA Cup*		*League Cup*	
	Apps	*Gls*	*Apps*	*Gls*	*Apps*	*Gls*
1969/70	40	10	9	2	0	0
1970/71	41	14	2	0	6	1
1971/72	44	19	4	3	1	0
1972/73	9(2)	0	1	0	1	0

Total (all competitions): 158(2) appearances, 49 goals

In total over all three spells: 248(2) appearances, 96 goals

13

Chesterfield

WITH Frank finding it difficult at Northampton, under pressure for not scoring, playing in the reserves, and admitting 'to being in a bit of a rut', out of the blue an offer came in from Jim McGuigan, manager of Third Division side Chesterfield. It was an offer that neither Frank nor Billy Baxter could afford to refuse, so Chesterfield became his ninth club.

A goalscoring debut in a 2-1 away win at Rochdale got him off to a wonderful start. He had failed to score in his previous 13 games in a struggling Northampton side that eventually had to apply for re-election that season.

The programme notes for Frank's home debut against Walsall on 2 February 1972 outlined McGuigan's reasons for getting his chequebook out. 'Since Ernie Moss dropped out with an ankle injury that necessitated an operation, our goal power left a lot to be desired. In Frank Large we think we have secured the right type of player to bring about a big improvement. He certainly made a good start at Rochdale and it was good to be back on the winning path in the league after five successive defeats.'

Another goal came in that game and a satisfying return of five goals in his first eight matches ensured that he was taken to by the Saltergate faithful.

As for the move my Dad stated, 'While it's been great, it was a bit unexpected when Chesterfield came after me, because I was all set to drop out of the league at the end of the season. I was going to work with a builder friend of mine, and in fact I have a house in the Midlands ready for my retirement.'

Frank's last few games for the Cobblers were for the reserves and he acknowledged, 'I was helping to bring on the youngsters in the second team, and just whiling away my time until Chesterfield came in for me. It made me feel very proud because at 32 and with all the clubs I'd had, you don't expect to start afresh again. But to be quite honest it's given me a new lease of life and I hope to continue to do well for them because they seem a really good club.'

The retirement house was in Deanshanger, in the south of Northamptonshire, and had just been fully renovated. Mum and Dad faced a final decision as to where we would end up being raised and for a while it looked like we would be moving back to Yorkshire, to the small market town of Otley just outside Leeds which was the hot favourite for some time.

Both Mum and Dad fancied moving back up north, and it sure suited me – the local paper mentions, 'One member of the Large household quite happy about the move to north-east Derbyshire is Frank's eldest son Paul (10).'

'Frank said, "It's the first time that one of my moves has affected my children's schooling for Paul is due to take his

11 Plus this year. But he was the first to say yes when I told the family that Chesterfield wanted me.

"Actually I couldn't have done anything if it hadn't been for my wife's support, she has been absolutely marvellous and never quibbled when we have had to pack up everything for another move. I've always asked her before agreeing and she's always realised it's for the best. Paul is so pleased because he's nearer Leeds – he's one of Leeds's keenest fans."

The article finished with an insight into Frank's direct opinion about going into management at the end of his playing career.

"With all the experience Large has picked up during his career – playing and living alongside players and managers of all creeds, wouldn't he like to stay in the game?' it asked.

"Certainly not," he replied. "You soon get old as a manager and I've seen everything that football has to offer. No I'll settle for working with my builder friend, it seems a nice quiet settled life."'

Mick Ward was the builder friend and much to my disappointment we didn't move north and Deanshanger became the family home for the next 15 years, an eternity in the Large history books!

As for Frank, logistically it wasn't going to be easy living 100 miles from your club.

The first casualty was the green Mini Clubman that so tickled the Cobblers lads. For the last time he bought a brand new car, a canary-yellow MK 3 Ford Cortina 1.6L. He travelled up to Chesterfield on the Monday, trained and then went up to my Grandma's (he initially stayed in digs in Chesterfield) in Leeds. He commuted the 45 miles every day until Thursday when he came home – just ready for the weekend match. With a lot of the teams in the south he often met the team at the away venue or joined them on the way.

As for home games, Richard and I went to every one. We got to know the town very well, especially the location of the Airfix model shops, the best of which was near the church with the surreal Dali-esque spire that dominates the town and from which the team gets its nickname.

We knew the gateman and he knew us so getting in was no problem. After the match we wandered back to the car park and climbed in to the unlocked car, and waited for Frank to appear, me being desperate to hear the result of Leeds United read by James Alexander Gordon on the BBC.

A colour pen photo of the time shows Frank leaning against a goalpost in his club shirt (a simple royal blue top with a round white collar and cuffs), holding a size five zephyr football, his hair brutally damped down, just as Graham Carr remembered, smiling at the camera.

Frank scored his 200th league goal against Swansea, and no surprises it was a header. After 60 minutes an Arthur Bellamy shot rattled the crossbar and with the Swansea goalkeeper Millington stranded Frank headed home.

Unfortunately he missed the next game, against his first club Halifax, but he would have been pleased to note that since his arrival, alongside the other new player, goalkeeper Jim Brown, the club had climbed to within six points of the top two.

Upon scoring his 200th goal Frank joined an elite list of only seven players active at that time who had achieved this landmark. The list included some of the game's great goalscoring characters: Ron Davies (Southampton), Ken Wagstaff (Hull), Tony Hateley (Oldham), Denis Law (Manchester United), Kevin Hector (Derby) and Derek Dougan (Wolves).

Sadly the season petered out and Chesterfield finished a disappointing 16th. The loss of key players through injury didn't help, but a shocking October proved disastrous. Frank's arrival helped and it was noted that 'Frank has given us fine service, and it is a pity that a lot of his good work has been wasted.'

The 1973/74 season started with a change of manager, with Joe Shaw taking the reins, and the return of the young tyro Ernie Moss. Three wins and two draws in the the first five games saw Frank score two and Ernie three. Despite an away defeat at Huddersfield the subsequent comprehensive victory over Blackburn left the Spireites flying near the top of the division.

Unfortunately Frank missed the next nine games with injury and despite playing through November and December he was injured again early in the New Year. From 1 January until 15 April he played only eight games and often struggled to make 90 minutes. As for Chesterfield, the free-scoring Moss enjoyed a good season and they eventually finished just outside the promotion places in fifth.

In researching this book I contacted the club and as always I was pleased with their willingness to help me in any way possible. They furnished me with a list of telephone numbers from some of the players from that era.

When I speak to Ernie I am immediately struck by the number of similarities between himself and Frank. Both were tough leaders of the line, both became legends at a club they played for three times, and both retired to non-league football at Kettering.

I ask him what was it like playing alongside Frank, 'Your Dad worked very hard, put in a lot of effort and always gave 100 per cent. He liked to mix it up and loved the physical challenge. I really enjoyed playing alongside him and learnt a lot.'

I ask him for any amusing stories or anecdotes, but he can't or won't recall any. However, he creases up when he remembers Albert Holmes's birthday party. I press but my Paxman-like skills are obviously lacking as he fails to spill the beans. We finish with a reflection of how unlucky they were that season and a brief re-cap of his own career, special mention going to Neil Warnock – a man that Ernie felt influenced him enormously.

Intrigued, I track down Albert Holmes to get the truth on the birthday party shenanigans. Although aged 68 he sounds 20 years younger, and when I mention Ernie's uncontrolled mirth at the events surrounding his party, he chuckles and tells me that Frank had managed to kill his daughter's goldfish when he carelessly discarded some lemons from his glass into the goldfish bowl. As Albert is laughing, I take it that it didn't upset his daughter too much and obviously Frank had been forgiven. It did sound like a good night and no cocktail waitresses or spit-roasting had been involved.

When Albert begins to tell me how nice Frank was, despite the fact that I've heard it so many times before my heart swells with pride. The respect of his peers always knocks me sideways, and by now I know it's genuine and heartfelt.

I ask him if he ever played against Frank, and he honestly can't remember, but then comes up with a cracker. 'Let me tell you,' he says quite seriously. 'I'd always sooner play with him than against him.'

We talk about his son's career and you feel the pride oozing out of him. Paul Holmes played with Torquay, Doncaster and Everton: 'He was never interested in becoming a pro, but got picked up playing with a local team and that was that.' Before I ask the question, I reckon I know the answer, 'Did he have a left foot ?' 'Oh aye, and a good right one too.'

Before I leave Albert in peace I ask him his opinion of the modern Premier League player and sadly his feelings appear to be common among his generation of journeyman pros, 'I wouldn't cross the road to watch a match.'

Frank played his last league match, his 629th game in professional English football, in a 2-0 defeat at Walsall on 15 April 1974 that marked the end of a long and interesting career in the Football League.

For us, at that time, the most significant event that season took place at the end of December when Frank was approached by the former Ipswich Town player Doug Millward, who was scouting for players to go to the USA to play in the re-established North American Soccer League.

Doug offered Frank a four-month contract to move with the family to Baltimore at the end of April, and turn out for – to us – the exotically-named Baltimore Comets.

The Phillips school atlas was taken down from the bookshelf and the North American continent scoured meticulously and so momentous was the occasion and so great the excitement we actually missed an episode of *The Sweeney* that Monday night, an unheard of event!

The subsequent four months took on a very different complexion as we counted down the days to our American adventure.

Frank Large's Chesterfield record

	League		*FA Cup*		*League Cup*	
	Apps	*Gls*	*Apps*	*Gls*	*Apps*	*Gls*
1972/73	23	9	0	0	0	0
1973/74	23	6	1	1	3	0

Total (all competitions): 50 appearances, 16 goals

14

USA

WE left England on 24 April 1974. London was cold and wet, and we were well wrapped up as we boarded the PanAm Boeing 747 Jumbo Jet to JFK New York, and then on to Baltimore.

No sooner were we seated and settled, just behind the first-class compartment, than the immaculately dressed cabin staff started to fuss over us – and they managed to keep it up for the full eight hours of the flight.

Shortly after take-off we realised that we were sharing the flight with a celebrity. Having won *Opportunity Knocks* for five weeks running and being the youngest person ever to have a UK top ten album, Lena Zavaroni was heading to Hollywood and a charity show with Frank Sinatra and Lucille Ball. Ten days younger than our Richard and happily wandering around the cabin signing autographs, it quickly became obvious she had taken a shine to our kid, as she walked past him several times. Richard just sat there mortified.

After landing in New York we waited for ages in the immigration line. Eventually we were called forward by a

6ft 6ins immigration officer who politely asked Frank the purpose of his visit. When Frank replied that he was there to play football a look of incredulous disbelief spread across the guy's broad features. 'You gotta be joking me?' he scoffed, and it appeared we were on our way back to Blighty. Only after intense scrutiny of visas and passports, along with a brief description of 'soccer', did he relent and let us in.

With the internal flight negotiated we only realised we were on a different continent when the club officials, who greeted us at the gate, escorted us to the waiting cars. Still swaddled in our many man-made layers we quickly began to melt in what was for us the scorching heat. The skies were clear and blue, the temperature was in the mid-70s, we were in a car bigger than a boat, everybody was polite and smiling, with wonderful teeth – happy days.

The apartment complex was in north Baltimore, a city famously described by film director Barry Levinson as 'pretty much a traffic jam between Washington and New York', close to the belt-way in the townsville of Pikesville.

Approximately a dozen blocks, with four apartments to each block, stood in landscaped gardens with a pool and hotel attached. Home for us, for the next four months, was on the first floor and was absolutely amazing; a large open-plan living and dining area, a massive balcony and a kitchen that every time I went in, I half expected to meet Raymond Baxter and a TV crew. It had microwave ovens, a dishwasher, massive fridge with an ice-box, waste disposal unit, extractor fan and an electric can opener.

The apartment also had three bedrooms and a bathroom with its own proper shower, not a Heath-Robinson rubber device you bunged on to the taps. However all this paled into insignificance when the 24-hours-a-day, 55-channel TV set was produced from behind its mahogany doors complete with a remote control. Trust me, in 1974 England this was science fiction.

Just before the officials left us to settle in and cope with the imminent arrival of our jet lag, they managed to get mine and Richard's attention away from the cartoon channel briefly by pointing out that the wooded area to the rear of the block should be avoided at all costs and at all times because of the poisonous snakes.

Suitably warned we returned to *The Flintstones* and thought no more about it. Some time later however, not ready for sleep yet, we excused ourselves (considerately allowing Mum and Dad to hunker down with David and Vicki) and outside we immediately found two sharp sticks, tucked our socks into our pants and headed for the prohibited woodland. Hours later we emerged gutted that we hadn't found a thing.

The next day we met one of the other English players the Comets hoped would secure success in the inaugural North American Soccer League – Kenny Hill, a 21-year-old centre-half from Gillingham, along with his wife Delia. They had no kids and were sharing our block, and immediately hit it off not just with our parents, but us kids as well.

Shortly, more club officials arrived to see if all was OK and then whisked Frank and Kenny off to the car pool to pick up the club cars. A couple of hours later Frank pulled into the parking space in a beautiful mustard-coloured Ford Mustang. Kenny followed in a red Ford Torino. We were in the back ready for a spin when Mum and Delia arrived.

After a cursory glance at the two+two seating arrangement in the Mustang, Mum pointed out the total impracticality of such a car for a married man with four kids. Crestfallen, Frank reluctantly swapped with Kenny, who took Delia off for a spin, leaving me and our kid devastated. Every day we looked at that car and wondered, if only.

The original plan was for us to go to school, but when we realised that they finished the year in four weeks it didn't seem worth it. So unbelievably we were on our holidays for four solid months – we tried hard to hide our disappointment.

The pool was situated next to the Quality Inn Hotel at the entrance to the complex. As was the custom the pool was filled with cold water in April and nature was left to warm it up. Most locals had no intention of going near it until the middle of June, when it was deemed suitable for use. They looked in amazement at the pasty foreigners cavorting in it in April. For us, it was warmer than the open-air baths in Wolverton ever got.

The other two English players recruited by team manager Doug Millward, a gruff Yorkshireman who had won a First Division championship with Alf Ramsey at Ipswich in the early 1960s, were both from Norwich City. They were Peter Silvester, a 26-year-old forward, and Geoff Butler, a 28-year-old full-back who Millward made club captain.

As the hastily-assembled squad prepared for their first game, Richard and I got the fantastic news that we were invited to be ball boys, dotted around the pitch for all the home matches. They didn't need to ask us twice. I had never got over the fact that we, as players' sons, were never allowed to be mascots at Northampton.

This was immense and we got our own uniform, with the club crest, a claret-coloured shooting comet, on the shirt and shorts, all topped off with three-quarter basketball socks. We were to be marshalled by a Poindexter lookalike, probably a director's son, who took his job far too seriously. The opportunity, however, to be so close to the action was special and to watch Frank up close was brilliant.

The Comets played their home matches at the Baltimore Memorial Stadium, shared with the much more famous baseball team the Orioles and the American football team the Colts. As a result the baseball diamond was cut into the football pitch and it was quite surreal to see the winger leave the grass as he screamed down the wing and go on to the cinders, before hitting the byline. Remarkably it didn't appear to affect the players too much, despite the noticeable two-inch drop. Frank did however get a few nasty gravel burns after being felled on the cinders.

As the first game approached the training got intense; hours were spent going over basic drills, simple instructions repeated adnauseam, and of course fitness improved. This wasn't the Comets, no, it was the ball boys and Poindexter was on a power trip, 'Wait until asked to throw on the ball, bounce it to the player, then go and retrieve.' Not exactly rocket science, but practice makes perfect and we tried to take it seriously.

As for the real deal, they were the usual NASL mix: a United Nations that included, along with the four Englishmen, four West Indians – wingers Keith Aqui and Al Henderson, full-back Winston Earle and goalkeeper Lincoln Phillips.

The rest of the team was comprised mainly of first- or second-generation Italian/Mexican/Polish-Americans,who had played soccer in college and lived locally. Many had played for the Baltimore Bays, the semi-professional predecessors to the Comets.

The template for the 1974 season saw the league completely rebooted, big time. Along with the Comets, seven other teams joined the competition – the Boston Minutemen, Denver Dynamos, Los Angeles Aztecs, San Jose Earthquakes, Seattle Sounders, Vancouver Whitecaps and the Washington Diplomats. There were four divisions: the Northern Division which included Boston, the Toronto Metros, Rochester Lancers and New York Cosmos; the Central Division comprised of just three teams, the Dallas Tornado, St Louis Stars and Denver Dynamos; the Western Division which was filled with the four new outfits from LA, San Jose, Seattle and Vancouver; while the Comets were in the Eastern Division along with the Miami Toros, Philadelphia Atoms and the Washington Diplomats.

A fiendishly complicated format saw all the teams play 20 matches; home and away against the teams in their division and in the case of the Comets, home and away against the teams in the Northern Division.

That accounted for 14 games. The other six appeared to be randomly picked and included St Louis and Dallas at home and San Jose and Los Angeles away.

The six teams with the most points at the end of the season qualified for the play-offs with the top two going straight into the semi-finals then third played sixth and fourth faced fifth.

If this wasn't complicated enough already, the points system would give you a headache! Six points were awarded for a win and three for a tie – draws were not allowed in the league so if after 90 minutes the scores were equal you went into a 'penalty-kick shoot-out' and if you won you got the three points for a tie. You also got one point for every goal scored up to a maximum of three.

The first match of that summer's campaign was played under lights on Wednesday 1 May, at home to the Rochester Lancers. The official attendance was 7,050 but many thousands more were enticed through the turnstiles as guests or through canny ticket promotions.

Tense and nervous, sitting under the main stand of the stadium, affectionally known as 'The Old Grey Lady of 33rd Street' or as the Colts fans preferred it 'The world's largest outdoor insane asylum', Richard and I prepared for the big night.

We weren't ready for what came next. This being the USA the players were never going to wander out swinging arms and lifting knees. As we sat waiting, the marching band and cheerleaders emerged from deep in the bowels of the main stand and marched out on to the pitch and performed for 15 minutes.

The fireworks display followed and finally the players, who were introduced individually over the PA system just like prize fighters, then had to run through the guard of honour to join their team-mates. Frank was introduced thus, '185lbs, from York...Shire, En..ger..land, Fraaaank Laarge'. Slightly bemused, he jogged to the centre circle and idly waited for the rest of the lads to join him.

We had been ushered into our positions and just as we thought there could not be any more delays the players were called to attention on the halfway line, and the National Anthem was sung. All and sundry placed their right hands on their left breast and sang with gusto, the only exceptions being me, our kid, Frank and Kenny.

At last the game kicked off! Being so close to the action was brilliant as you could definitely hear the players and you flinched when the challenges went in; your arms, legs and neck moved involuntarily as you kicked and headed every ball. The sweat and steam coming off the players heightened your senses, and it was all magnified by the fact that we were outside under floodlights, with a 52-piece marching band playing inane music. Unforgettable.

As half-time approached the ball left the pitch and bounced towards Richard, who was 20 yards away from me on the touchline. Without hesitation he controlled the ball on his chest and volleyed it back to the approaching Lancer.

Back under the main stand during the break Poindexter went apoplectic, ranting and raving about not following instructions. As he launched into another round of abuse I snapped at him to fucking shut up!

Not used to the Queen's English being delivered in such a succinct manner by a skinny ginger-haired 11-year-old, it did the trick and he said no more. A Mexican stand-off ensued, where he refused to talk to us and we just took the piss out of him knowing we would be quickly replaced and would have to get used to watching the rest of the season from the 'big stand' three-quarters of a mile away.

Funnily enough, two games later it was him who left with no explanation, and we got to enjoy all the perks of being ball boys for the summer. Mind you Richard didn't try any more fancy stuff and we did as we were told.

As for the Comets it was a winning start, Pete Silvester scoring both goals in a 2-1 victory. After the match we realised that not only were we allowed to wander into the dressing room after tidying the bibs and balls away, we were also allowed access to the free vending machine – ice-cold Coke and Pepsi for free.

We then followed the players, carrying kit bags and trying to look both important and busy, into the lounge, where club directors, their families and the players' families were all gathered in a function room that resembled a wedding in a posh hotel. There was a buffet of food and a free bar from which waiters brought pitchers of beer and nibbles to the tables. The atmosphere was very friendly and introductions and glad-handing deemed very important as not only the players but their wives and families were made welcome by the hierarchy of the club.

As the pitchers ran dry we were dispatched to go and get them refilled (the beer was sponsored by the local brewery, which was clearly visible from the stadium). We duly did, our commission being a few stolen swigs, taken not because we liked it but because we could!

The treatment of the families was light years ahead of what was happening in England at that time, where most clubs would reluctantly provide a couple of free match tickets (non-refundable) to the players and players' lounges in the lower leagues were still as rare as hen's teeth. A few days later the team flew to New York to take on the Cosmos. This was a couple of years before the 'Galacticos' appeared on the New York soccer scene, when the arrival of Pele, Beckenbauer and Carlos Alberto in the country's bicentennial year not only graced the NASL but made the club world-famous.

But a 3-2 victory with Silvester netting two more and Acqui getting the third made for a great end to their first week in the league.

As Frank settled into life as a Comet, our life adapted quickly to a cycle of shopping malls, Howard Johnsons, McDonalds, swimming, messing and the TV. Having got close to Kenny and Delia we often went off on days out, visiting Ocean City and Gettysburg, Richard and I even getting to ride in the rear of the Mustang. The days were long, hot and dry and having made friends with some of the other kids who lived on the complex we had a great time.

We learned not to call cigarettes 'fags', started talking about 'black' people as opposed to referring to them as 'coloured', as we had always done thinking that it was polite, and generally immersed ourselves in a culture that was so different, energetic, positive and exciting.

We even went to a baseball match. David had made friends with the sons of the Baltimore Orioles legend Mark Belanger, the short-stop who had helped them win the World Series in 1970. That feat had gone unnoticed in our house as we focussed on the drama unfolding in Mexico.

Mark lived across the way from us and in front of a capacity crowd of 48,000 in the Memorial Stadium we sat for five long hours – it was a double-header of games – and saw one home run. It was a tad boring, but the constant flow of popcorn, hot dogs and fizzy drinks eased the burden. That experience was enough for me and Richard, we and didn't go again despite a number of invitations.

A 3-2 home defeat to the Philadelphia Atoms in which all five goals were scored by Brits (two for David Provan for the Atoms and one for Jim Fryatt, with Butler and Silvester scoring for the Comets) saw the Earthquakes arrive in Baltimore only to get thrashed 6-2, Frank opening his account across the 'pond' with a brace.

Frank scored another goal in a 3-2 win over the Boston Minutemen but picked up an injury that forced him to miss the next match, a crushing 4-1 loss to the same opposition, before he returned for the 2-0 win over the local rivals, the Washington Diplomats.

The team's form was erratic to say the least, a home defeat to St Louis Stars followed by two more on the road in Toronto and Miami. One consolation was that Frank was finding the net, with five goals in his nine appearances to date.

An injury to the Caribbean custodian Phillips allowed 21-year-old New Yorker Alan Mayer a chance to impress. The draft pick was one of the few players who took time out to get to know us ball boys and deserved all the success he subsequently achieved – Alan followed the Comets franchise as it criss-crossed the continent. Over the next few years, they became the San Diego Jaws in 1976, then the Las Vegas Quicksilver in 1977 before returning to San Diego as the Sockers in 1978. Alan was named the NASL American Player of the Year in 1978 and gained six caps for the USA.

I recall one conversation with him, concerning music when he was asking me, a 12-year-old who was not really interested in music, who we liked and who was big in the UK. Never one to duck a challenge, I spoofed that Slade were the bees' knees and was genuinely shocked that he hadn't heard of them. When asked about his favourites I remember laughing out loud when he said the Beatles. The irony of course was that summer, Paul McCartney and Wings had the number one album *Band on the Run* which was never off the wireless (along with the Watergate scandal and the impeachment of Nixon) and formed the soundtrack to our stay. Even today when I hear the clanging guitars of the introduction I am taken back to Maryland.

Alan was a really nice lad who had a super-cool mid-1960s Mustang, and yes we did get to go out in it for a spin.

We only saw two away matches that season. One was a 6-0 humiliation in the Robert F. Kennedy Stadium, Washington, when the Diplomats ran riot and poor Alan made his final appearance between the sticks. The other was a memorable trip to Philadelphia.

For an approximately 85-mile trip north of Baltimore, some bright spark felt that a bright yellow school bus just like Otto's in *The Simpsons* was an appropriate vehicle in which to make the journey.

Apart from scoffing at the obvious inadequacies of the ball boys, we enjoyed the match, a 1-1 draw the Comets got three points for as a result of winning the shoot-out.

Happy, we returned to the bus and as we set off the driver realised that the doors wouldn't shut and after ten minutes of increasingly agitated fumbling he gave up attempting to fix them so we set off home. Two hours later, numb and with the first stages of frostbite, we arrived back.

The 198th 4 July celebrations saw the club organise a party for all the playing staff and their families. We had been to a number of the club directors' homes and they were very plush and well appointed but this one was the best house I had ever been in, and remains so to this day. Situated in a posh suburb outside the city in lovely rolling countryside, this house had the obligatory pool, tennis and basketball court – and its own baseball pitch.

Inside was similarly impressive but the *piece de resistance* was the den. Occupying the complete basement this room had it all; pool table, table football, a bar, leather sofas, an enormous TV and a VCR the size of a large suitcase which cost a mere $3,000.

Highlights of that summer's World Cup were being screened. Having watched the 30-second montage of Leeds United's brave attempt to lift the trophy for Scotland, I wandered out for a game of baseball, happy with the thought that the collective experience of playing at the highest level would guarantee another successful season for David Harvey, Gordon McQueen, Frank Gray, Billy Bremner, Peter Lorimer, Eddie Gray and Joe Jordan. Along with a new manager things could only get better.

That day was amazing and the celebrations extraordinary – the fireworks, barbecues, music, entertainment, flags and pride was overwhelming. I have never seen anything like it since and consider myself very fortunate to have been there.

With the Comets looking good for a play-off berth despite the season's ups and downs, Frank was approached by the club regarding his options for next season and he tacitly agreed to return in a player-coach position. I remember him discussing it with Mum, and being asked for my opinion on it. When I realised that the club were looking for Frank to move permanently to Baltimore I was delighted and let them know it.

Many English players were making a good living in the States by extending their careers and moving into coaching and management, but Frank was reluctant and his experience over the years in England with clubs and managers saying one thing and doing another made him cautious. He was never a 'political animal' and couldn't stand hypocrites either and always spoke his mind; three good reasons for avoiding a career in football management. Family considerations were also discussed and while it remained an option I knew we were going home. I was disappointed, but got over it.

The Comets finished second in the Eastern Division with the third highest number of points, just missing out on automatic qualification to the semi-finals, having won ten, lost eight and tied two. Frank managed a return of nine goals in his 18 games, not bad for a 34-year-old. The next game was crucial because if they won and then got past the semi, we would have got another two weeks in the States. Lose and we got packing. The opposition were the Minutemen, who finished sixth, and the quarter-final was played in Boston on 15 August. The 1-0 defeat was Frank's last professional game and we left the States a few days later.

Pete Silvester deservedly won the league's Most Valuable Player award. Kenny and Delia had become good friends and we remained in touch for a number of years.

After 15 years and four months Frank was now an ex-professional footballer, having played 648 games and scored 235 goals in total for all of his clubs.

The Comets started the 1975 season at the Memorial Stadium before being kicked out mid-term for non-payment of rent and at the end of the campaign they headed west.

The departure of the Comets pre-dated the much more upsetting loss to the city nine years later of the Colts. The flamboyant owner Bob Irsay sneaked the American football club out of the city overnight in a fleet of lorries, pitching up in Indianapolis one snowy night in 1984, leaving only the marching band's uniforms behind, which were at the cleaners.

Snapping at a TV reporter before the move, Irsay said, 'It's not your club, it's not our club, it's my club. I paid for it.' The reaction of the supporters was immediate and emotional, but ultimately futile.

The wilderness years for the fans ended when controversially the Cleveland Browns relocated to Baltimore, as the 'Ravens' and in a new stadium.

This approach to football as business is here already, and while the abomination that is Milton Keynes Dons is bad enough, the shenanigans at Cardiff City and Hull City do not bode well for the future of our national game – but then again you can call me old-fashioned.

Back to 1974 and we got back to Church Lane, Deanshanger, to be greeted with a burst water tank and a collapsed ceiling – holiday over. Still, beautifully sun-tanned I looked forward to getting back to school, safe in the knowledge that I would keep the most amazing memories of the best experience of my life forever. Frank got his work clothes out and headed for a building site in Northampton, that Monday morning.

Frank always saw football as a job. Enjoyable and well-paid at times, but ultimately just a way of paying the bills and as he had no inclination to stay in the game after retirement, he knew he had to find another way to look after the family.

With no qualifications he knew it would be labouring. It didn't phase him, and as with all things he took it in his stride and got on with it.

Frank Large's Baltimore Comets record

	League	
	Apps	*Gls*
1974	18	9

Total (all competitions): 18 appearances, 9 goals

15

Kettering Town

I FIRST contacted Ron Atkinson in the mid-1990s when he was managing Coventry City in the Premier League. My Mum and Dad had lost a legal case over a right of way with the neighbour from hell, who made The Bull McCabe look like Mother Teresa! The costs were quite high and I thought that if I could organise a testimonial it might help with the bill.

Sadly but predictably Northampton Town failed to respond in any way, yet Ron called me back that very afternoon as soon as he came in off the training ground. After I explained the situation, he not only offered the use of his first XI but also some other big names he could press-gang. When I mentioned that Northampton appeared lukewarm he even suggested the possible use of Highfield Road.

It didn't get any further, and Mum and Dad eventually went to the credit union, but Ron's time and generous offer was heart-warming.

Frank signed for Ron's Southern League outfit Kettering Town in the autumn of 1974, shortly after we returned from the States. Trevor Gould allegedly spotted him on a building site and asked if he was interested in earning a few extra bob. Frank was grateful for the opportunity.

Alan Poole was a local journalist at the time and covered Kettering during Frank's only season in non-league football. He wrote the following article shortly after Frank died and it brilliantly sums up what he meant to his legions of fans who adored his never-say-die attitude on the pitch.

I contacted Alan for permission to use his article, and he kindly agreed saying it would be an honour – the following appeared in the *Coventry Telegraph* in August 2003:

> 'He ended up 20 miles along the A43 when he was recruited by Ron Atkinson to bolster Kettering Town's push for the Football League.
>
> 'It didn't pay off (those were the days before automatic promotion, when the so-called annual election process was an old pals' stitch-up in a smoggy antechamber of the Cafe Royal) and Big Ron soon departed to Cambridge United for the next stage of the journey that would take him to Old Trafford.
>
> 'But Atkinson, a man who revelled in his playing nickname "The Tank", relished his short spell with a football warrior after his own heart. And even though he bought, sold and controlled some of the finest talents to grace the British game that respect and affection remains undiminished.
>
> 'Frank was terrific to work with. Atkinson confirmed, "He was as strong as a lion and as competitive as any player I've ever known. He worked on the building sites and I remember him coming in one

day when he had dropped a hod of bricks on his foot and broken his big toe. He knew we were a bit short, so he just cut a chunk out of his boot to make it a bit more comfortable so he could play.

'"He used to tell me that the only player he was ever scared of on a football field was Johnny Haynes, and that was when they were in the same team at Fulham!

'"Johnny was always bawling him out for one thing or another, but make no mistake Frank was a bloody good player. If he was around today clubs would be flocking around to sign him up."

'Thirty years ago when I was covering Kettering for another *Evening Telegraph* I cornered Frank in the home dressing room at Rockingham Road while we were waiting for the team bus that would ferry us to Dover for a Tuesday night Southern League match.

'I was looking for a nice background piece on the Poppies' latest acquisition, but I was a bit concerned about how I could get hold of his convoluted career details: in those days we didn't have the internet databases at our fingertips and the office copy of the Rothmans invariably went walkabout within a week.

'No problem, within a minute of the introduction formalities being completed, Frank launched into a comprehensive verbal CV – transfer dates, appearances and goal tallies, reeled off in the dry Yorkshire monotone that never deserted him throughout his football wanderings.

'It wasn't conceit, it was consideration – professional courtesy from a man who tackled all his responsibilities with a working class craftsman's attention to detail. And it was utterly enthralling.

'My second endearing memory of Large was another midweek match this time against Wimbledon, who were then in the process of overhauling Kettering & co as the prime contenders for that elusive passport to the League.

'Although they were building up a reputation as romantic giant-killers on the national scene, they fancied themselves as big-time "Charlies" at their own level, swaggering around like city slickers deigning to drop in for a brief audience with the country bumpkins.

'And one of their main attractions was Roger Connell, a lolloping centre-forward who looked like a Grateful Dead roadie, and had what could fairly be described as an unfortunate manner.

'That night he was giving Frank, playing at centre-half for the Poppies, all manner of physical and verbal aggravation, and in due course he strutted up to his veteran marker, chest puffed up and heavily bearded jaw thrust out in the time-honoured manner of masculine confrontation.

'A split-second later he was flat on his back, pole-axed by a right jab that combined minimum backlift with maximum impact as neatly as any boxer could have contrived. And an instant after that, Large swivelled on his heels and strode to the tunnel, sparing the referee the formality of a red and ensuring that the incident did not escalate into a mass brawl.

'Now of course you shouldn't try this at home, and I'm not suggesting that a flash of irrefutably violent conduct is a fitting memorial to one of football's great characters.

'But compared to the squealing shenanigans dished up by that gaggle of sporting millionaires in Cardiff the other day, it had a certain savage dignity, even nobility.

'And in its own strange way, trust me, it was really rather beautiful.'

My brother and I were in the main stand and I remember clearly the Wimbledon player approaching Dad, mouthing obscenities as he walked on to a perfect uppercut that actually lifted him off his feet. As he hit the deck the 3,000 or so supporters in the main stand rose as one and roared and cheered as if they had won the cup final.

David Thorpe, then of the *Eastern Daily Press*, remembers interviewing Frank after that match, 'Outside the dressing rooms later, I meekly asked if Connell might have made a meal of the fall. "Did he heck as like," boomed Frank, raising the offending fist. "That was the most perfect punch you'll ever see. I knocked him cold."'

David also recalls that the then Wimbledon player Dave Bassett also had an altercation with Frank. 'I approached Bassett and Wimbledon manager Allen Batsford as they headed for the clubhouse after a 2-0 defeat seen by a crowd of just under 4,000. One of Bassett's hands was swathed in bandages and when I asked why he snapped, "Frank Large bit it! He's taken a bloody great chunk out." Again Frank made no attempt to deny the accusation. When asked if Bassett was telling the truth he responded with a smile. "All I can say is, what was his hand doing in my mouth?"'

Having secured Big Ron's number I contact him on a cold and wet February afternoon. The call is answered but the reception is terrible and I am just about to give up when it clears and the familiar voice becomes recognisable, 'Sorry about that, it's a bit windy outside.' True to form he is at his apartment in Tenerife and off the sun lounger.

With the introductions over he is keen to talk about Frank and reels off the anecdotes, most of which he mentions in his book. The story about having to stop the bus for the smokers, Frank being one of them, is recalled, and I point out that my Dad never smoked in his life. Ron laughs, 'Yes he did, of course he did. There were three or four of them, I am sure your Dad was one of them.'

I tell him I remember him cutting the front of his boot off in our kitchen with a Stanley knife the night he played with the broken big toe, and ask if he got a cortisone injection to ease the pain. Again the familiar laugh, this time followed with a one-liner for which he is justly famous. 'A cortisone injection, back then the lads thought that was some kind of fancy foreign car! We gave him a slug of whiskey and out he went. He was great your Dad, he told me he had to take a couple of years off as they had got a big contract on the buildings in London, and I remember telling him that he'd be nearly 38 by then, so I persuaded him to stay and play.'

We reminisce some more and talk about my Dad's former Cobblers colleague Joe Kiernan, who had recently died.

Sensing that the sun was calling Ron I thank him for his time, and he kindly offers me any further assistance should I need it.

Just as we complete our goodbyes he comes out with a classic line, 'Your Dad was a one-man Captain Custer.' Laughing, he cuts off the call and presumably heads off to the beach.

I am laughing as well, then it dawns on me that what he had said didn't make any sense at all. I continue to laugh because of course I understood it, and surely that's the point. Frank thought very highly of Ron Atkinson, telling me on more than one occasion that he was the best manager he ever worked with. 'He could really motivate you, he'd get the adrenaline pumping before the game,' he would say. Frank wasn't surprised at how far Ron went in the game and always remembered his playing days at Kettering fondly.

That season they won the Southern League Cup and along with his two Third Division championship medals, Frank secured only three pieces of silverware in a 16-year career.

Frank threw his kit bag in the shed and while I wish I could tell you that his boots are in a glass case in my study the truth is more mundane. I managed to stuff the toes with cotton wool and wore them out playing for the school and village team in the mid-1970s.

They are probably in a landfill site outside of Milton Keynes, along with his Baltimore Comets tracksuit (which I lived in for a couple of years). What would I pay for them on eBay today!

16

Deanshanger

THE summer of 1976 was probably the best one I'll ever live to see. The sun never stopped shining and the heat was unbelievable, while we had six weeks off school and no exams.

It was the year Frank entered the factory having had enough of commuting to London to work on the buildings. He had a good friend in the personnel manager Cyril Nicholls who engineered the start.

Adolf Hitler was ultimately responsible for the oxide works, the red factory that dominated the village of Deanshanger. Abraham Wreshner, a German Jew, spotted the way the wind was blowing in the early 1930s and with his wife Hersha and two sons Kurt and Hans, fled the Nazis and turned up in Deanshanger in 1935, buying the derelict A.H. Roberts Iron foundry, which had stood on the spot since 1820.

In partnership with the London firm Morris Ashby, the site was converted to the production of iron oxide. It proved to be extremely profitable for a number of decades as the pigment production process took place in very few other places around the world, and utilised cheap waste products from other industries.

After internment during the war on the Isle of Man, the Wreshners returned to the village and ran the company themselves until selling it to Harrison Crossfield in 1982 when it was renamed Deanox. The factory finally closed in the late 1990s, a direct result of the rise of China as an economic powerhouse and its ability to make the oxide considerably cheaper. So the factory grew as a result of European fascism and shut as a result of international communism.

In the middle of that summer of 1976's heatwave Frank joined the day shift, clocking in at 7.30am following a brisk five-minute walk that took him through the picturesque heart of the village, past the green and the Wreshner mansions, before reaching the Dickensian factory and its forbidding gates.

That year we had effectively set up camp on the green, and rolling Test matches of 20 innings were played out between the top of the village and us, the bottom, play being suspended in mid-afternoon allowing us to cycle to Passenham and swim in the River Ouse.

On his lunchbreak Frank rounded the corner at the green, heading for home, head down and walking hard. Our kid and I temporarily abandoned our positions in the deep and scampered over to get his first reactions to working in the factory, a place that until that day, although it dominated the village and turned your washing red (if the wind was blowing in the wrong direction!), we had no relationship with and knew next to nothing about.

As we approached it became obviously apparent that he wasn't too happy and as we dropped into step behind him we realised that something was very wrong. Always a man of few words, that day Frank remained tight-lipped, our innocent questions going unanswered.

Following him into the kitchen we noticed he had a red hue on his hands, face and most noticeably, around his eyes, which looked like badly applied mascara – red oxide dust, the factory's produce, which despite overalls and masks permeated every pore.

In response to Mum's question, 'Well how was it?' Frank threw down his lunchbox and stated calmly but forcefully, 'I am not fucking going back in that shithole!' Realising this wasn't a conversation for all the family we were shooed out of the back door and sauntered back to the green to resume our fielding positions.

I remember worrying what he would do if he didn't go back as he'd had enough of working on the buildings and there wasn't a massive demand for a former centre-forward with no formal qualifications, and kept an eye out for him should he change his mind. Sure enough at five to two he trudged into view, threw us a quick nod and disappeared back around the corner into the factory – where for the next 11 years he provided for us all until he left Deanshanger, and England, forever.

Come 1977, I was desperate for a summer job and Frank put in a good word with Cyril and I too walked through those gates for the first time. I had to lie about my age, moving my birthday forward by 30 days, making me 15 and eligible to work the full six weeks of the holidays as a casual day labourer – a summer job I kept for the next ten years.

Already a regular for the village football team, Deanshanger Athletic, I was quickly alerted to the fact that the factory had an occasional friendly match against McCorquodales Printers from Wolverton. That summer's match was coming soon with the factory team organised by the manager of the local village team. So naturally, despite my callow youth, I confidently (if a little arrogantly) expected to participate fully.

The fact that Frank had agreed to play didn't elicit much reaction from me until the actual day arrived. As I polished my Adidas Valencias, leather boots with a vinyl covering that used to peel off, with red flashing, bought annually from the Grattans catalogue, I realised that I would actually be playing with Frank.

As the day progressed my nerves gradually grew and grew, the anticipation unbearable and the butterflies in my stomach nearly making me sick. I couldn't wait for it to begin, this wasn't just a friendly for pipe-fitters, storemen, forklift drivers and the like, this was my chance to play alongside my hero, my dad, Frank Large. I had spent the last ten years watching him play, now I would get the chance to play alongside him.

As I took my seat the banter in the changing room was the usual mix of mickey-taking, sarcasm, wild exaggerations and lewd comments that anyone who has ever played the game would enjoy, chip in on and miss like hell when they can no longer participate. I know I was the butt of many of them, 15 and daddy's boy! I am also sure I either chose not to notice, or didn't understand, but I certainly didn't join in – that right was yet to be earned.

The powerful smell of horse liniment for the pre-match rub, mingled with stale sweat and cigarette smoke, clogged the back of my throat. My preparation had been meticulous and the boots with tie-ups (laces nicked out of my brother's shoes) were placed on the cool tile floor and a massive pair of nylon shorts were flung at me.

Socks followed and I sat there quietly watching the rituals of the other players, most of whom I knew. I noticed that Frank had accepted a battered pair of old boots, and I briefly regretted wearing his pair out. As the liniment was passed around the offensive liquid was poured on to thighs which were then vigorously massaged to get the blood flowing. This constituted the warm-up. 'Not quite Old Trafford, Frank, eh?' 'No that's a fact,' he retorted as he began a number of stretches, squats and twists. I then copied the same routine for the next 20 years.

At last with just minutes to go, the manager produced the team sheet, a scrag-end of a bookies slip, and my stomach tightened another notch and my bowels clenched involuntarily. The manager proceeded to detail the formation and I tried to relax as the back line was divulged.

When he named the right-winger I realised he had made a mistake, but, with no need to panic, quickly anticipated his master plan – he intended to play us, me and Frank, up top. Frank's aerial ability and experience alongside my pace and energy. As I pondered this thought, the forwards were named and I was thrown the number 13 shirt and would be starting on the bench.

I felt physically sick and my eyes started watering. I struggled to hide the massive disappointment and pulled on the Bukta jersey that was made out of the same material as pan scrubs. The experienced players applied a final coating of Vaseline on their nipples and we were ready to go.

I was still in shock and could not begin to understand what had happened. I knew I was better than half of those selected but could do nothing about it. The manager sensed this and rubbed his hand over my head as he passed. I wanted to grab that hand and break every fucking finger, the bastard didn't even know what he had done! Without a team talk we headed out into a beautiful summer's evening – and as we left fags were stubbed out on the frame of the changing room door, others taking to giving it a good kick in a strange act of random violence.

All shapes and sizes were there and the mixture of beer bellies, shirts tucked in, shirts left out, shorts rolled up (revealing massive white, hairless thighs), crew-cuts and lank locks made this team the most unprofessional you ever saw – that was until the opposition emerged with a real old-school look, 'odd socks and plimsolls'.

One player out of the 22, however, stood out, the barrel chest and shock of blond hair as distinctive as ever. Having retired two years earlier and now aged 37, Frank still looked every bit the professional he once was, even in his borrowed, scuffed and unpolished boots and ill-fitting shorts.

The referee arrived and with the formalities over, the ball was placed on the bare centre spot, the whistle blown and the game began. I was stood on the touchline; no dug-out, no tracksuit, and miserable as sin.

The game resembled many that I had already played in and would go on to play in – a low level of skill and technique, overly compensated by hard work and effort. The ball barely touched the tufts of grass that formed isolated islands in the bare strip of earth that ran through the middle of the pitch, joining both goalmouths. Fortunately the pitch was also a part of the cricket outfield and at least it had been rolled. The wings however were more lush and with the grass cut short, if you squinted, it did resemble a football pitch, despite the occasional puffs of dust kicked up as the players chased over the barren expanses.

The opening exchanges were uneventful and neither goal was threatened. With both teams pushing up to get the offside, the play was condensed into the middle third of the park. Frank barely touched the ball and his intelligent running off it, looking to create space and opportunity, was lost on his team-mates. Their only plan appeared to be to 'lift it and shift it' over the top. Unimpressed, I convinced myself that if I was on the wing I could scamper down the touchline and deliver the perfect ball for Frank to score his 236th goal.

A full-back hoofed a hopeful ball in Frank's general direction and despite the close attention of two heavyweight defenders, he climbed and controlled the ball on his chest, swivelled in the air and laid it off perfectly into the channel for the right-winger to attack. Which he would have done (I would have done!) if he hadn't been stood on his heels, on the halfway line, hands on hips, puffing like a steam train.

Twenty minutes in and the game was opening up, the breathing was deeper and the faces were redder. Frank latched on to a bouncing through-ball and from fully 30 yards he sent an arcing shot that the keeper just managed to tip over. This was more like it!

The guy marking him was not sure what to do, whether to get tight or sit off, and as was beginning to wish he could mark someone else, the corner was taken and the number nine shirt jumped unchallenged and the blond head powered the ball back across the goal into the top corner for 1-0.

Laughing, he turned towards his own goal and stoop-shouldered walked back up the pitch. Exalted and bursting with pride, I temporarily forgot my injustices and clapped enthusiastically. I might have even smiled at the manager.

A few more deft touches and a powerful run and shot saw Frank get through to half-time in good shape. The quartered oranges were produced on the pitch and the manager, fag in hand, checked for any injuries. I hovered impatiently, praying that one of them had had enough and couldn't face another 45 minutes. Buoyed by their success and obviously keen to piss me off, not one of them fell on his sword and the second half began with me even more desolate, still on the sideline.

Ten minutes in, I watched as another long ball was lobbed over the top and as Frank collected it he started to bear down on goal. What happened next appeared to occur in slow motion.

Galloping towards the edge of the box, eyes fixed on the ball, he began to tilt forward and suddenly collapsed head first into the dry and dusty ground. He didn't even appear to be able to get his hands out to break the fall and I began to fear that he might have seriously hurt himself.

The group of concerned players huddled around from both teams appeared to confirm this. However as I was about to run on he rose slowly and started to walk gingerly to the touchline. A brief nod to the manager was enough and I was told to get ready.

Smiling and a tad embarrassed, he left the pitch just as I stepped on – and for just one brief glorious second, I had two feet on the same pitch as Frank – team-mates!

Then he was gone and he never stepped on to a football pitch again as a player. As he made his way to the changing rooms, thinking no doubt of a way to explain to Mum the cuts and bruises, there were no handshakes, no fanfare, no photographs or autographs, no nothing – just the way he would have wanted it.

17

Ireland

THE move to Ireland in the mid-1980s came completely out of the blue. I always reckoned that Mum and Dad would end up in Spain and while I knew we had an Irish connection (on my mother's side, Granddad spoke with a funny accent and had 12 kids!), and had visited in the mid-1960s, I didn't have a clue as to where they lived, let alone keep in touch.

The phone call came in late 1986 when my parents had just got back from a holiday in the west of Ireland and had fallen in love with a derelict cottage, with two lakes and 40 acres of land. It was in the shadow of Ireland's Holy Mountain, Croagh Patrick, on the Atlantic coast of County Mayo. With Dad not being one to mess around the house was soon on the market and the move completed by July 1987.

I was impressed with their courage and felt proud and optimistic that at 47 years old, Frank was taking this massive step. He had done 11 years in the factory and being on shifts and working long hours was taking its toll. All three of us sons had worked in the factory and experienced the Dickensian feel of the dirty, dusty work environment and the sheer monotony of the toil. I was delighted that he was getting out.

The 40-foot container was filled to bursting point and we set off to Holyhead and the overnight boat to Dun Laoghaire. Somewhat bleary-eyed we arrived at a ridiculously early hour and decided to push on.

A few hours later we pulled into a small-sized town, looking for a cup of tea and some breakfast. It was unimaginably dull, drab and depressing. Nothing was open (it was now past 9am) and I turned to Frank and told him that if he chose to live somewhere like this, he would not be seeing me again in a hurry.

As we left Longford, the monotonous, flat, nondescript bog-land started to change and a line of mountains appeared in the far distance to our right. The sun even began to shine and my spirits were immediately lifted.

As we approached Westport and Sheeaun, Frank took his foot off the accelerator, allowing me more time to take in the most amazing view. The mountain range on our right raced down to the sea and formed the northern boundary of Clew Bay which was shimmering on the horizon.

The monstrous hulk of Claire Island sat in the middle dominating the bay and its myriad of islands, and to our left the beautiful, near-perfect conical mass of the Reek (Croagh Patrick) rose majestically to 2,500ft, framing the view perfectly. As we raced down the hill Westport appeared to nestle in the shadow of the mountain, though this was an illusion as it was five miles out of town, and unlike all of the towns we had passed through since leaving Dublin, this one had character; more than just one street, beautifully laid out, the Georgian buildings gave the town a harmony that few other towns in Ireland possess. While familiar, it was also exotic and vaguely foreign, definitely not like Longford. 'Well what do you reckon? Frank asked. I just smiled.

Without stopping we climbed out of the town and headed inland towards the mountain which completely dominates the surroundings. Just five minutes out of town we stopped at a little track that led off the main road, between two small lakes, over a bridge to an old house sitting on a small hillock in the middle of a sea of heathery bog. The Reek was behind and to the right, no more than three miles to the summit, the well-worn 'Pilgrim's Path' clearly visible, as is the little church nestled on the top.

Local legend has it that while on the summit for 40 days St Patrick not only fought the Devil, but also banished all serpents from Ireland. On the last Sunday in July tens of thousands of pilgrims climb the mountain to attend Mass, in the church, the only day of the year it is open.

With great pride Frank announced 'We are here' and sped up the track towards the cottage.

We took a quick tour as Mum investigated the 40-foot static caravan that would be home for the next year. As Frank outlined the work that needed to be done I realised that without water or electricity this wasn't a simple refurbishment and I was aware that Frank's building skills were somewhat limited. However I could see the potential and Mum and Dad's energy and enthusiasm for the project convinced me that this new venture would be a great success.

And so it was. Gradually over the years the house was extended, a bed and breakfast business evolved (looked after very successfully by Mum), grass was cut and trees were planted. Having retired, Frank got himself a job at the world-famous Delphi Fishing Lodge as a handyman, a role he enjoyed for the best part of 12 years, before his illness forced him to have to pack it in.

Peter and Jane Mantle, having taking on a slightly bigger renovation challenge than Mum and Dad at around the same time, had bought the derelict hunting and fishing lodge (formerly owned by the Marquis of Sligo), a sizeable Georgian pile, wedged between Finlough and Doolough on the world-famous salmon river the Bundorragha.

Along with 2,500 acres and a half of Connacht's highest mountain, Mweelrea, the estate graced the Mayo–Galway border in Connemara, and Frank loved working there, in the wild outdoors. No two days were the same, and he liked that. Peter and Jane were great employers and I don't reckon Frank was ever happier after his days of terrorising centre-halves and goalkeepers.

Having moved to Westport three years later in the summer of 1990, I had the pleasure and honour of managing two local senior football teams with Frank.

Leaving England with a baby daughter, reluctant wife and no job was no easy decision, but the fact that Frank had secured me the player-manager job at Westport United helped make the move a little less traumatic.

At the first training session more than 40 lads turned up looking to impress the new management team on a lovely evening at The Point, a finger of land sticking out into Clew Bay, with the sea on three sides – surely one of the most picturesque practice grounds on the planet.

We quickly whittled the squad down to a more manageable number and Frank's experience was invaluable as we set about moulding a team to compete in the Connaught Senior League.

I tended to do most of the talking as Frank wasn't comfortable addressing the players *en masse*, he much preferred to talk quietly, one to one and his shrewd observations generally produced results. The forwards and goalkeepers particularly prospered as he took them for separate sessions.

With me being on the pitch, his sparse comments at half-time were god-sent. A wink here and a nod there was all he needed to do. One ploy we used was the fact that, as trainer, Frank could gain access to the pitch, with a bucket of cold water and sponge at the ready. I regularly needed attention (especially in the second half when substitutes might be ready to appear!) and on ran Frank to tell me who to remove and what to change, if anything, before dousing me, usually down the back of my shirt, with the freezing cold water out of the magic sponge.

He was also a dab hand with injuries. A clash of heads one afternoon left me bleeding quite badly above the eye, and the recent introduction of the 'blood rules' meant I had to leave the pitch until it stopped bleeding. With the sponge, plasters and Vaseline failing to do the job and no chance of a couple of stitches, I resigned myself to the fact that, frustratingly, my game was over.

Undeterred, Frank reached down into the muck and scooped up a thumbful of mud. Carefully he pushed and packed the mud into the open wound and, hey presto, it stopped bleeding and I could get back into the action. No doubt this was an old trick he had picked up decades ago but washing it out after wasn't so nice!

Many a long journey around the province was shared and it was a treat to be in his company, being involved with football. He never showed any frustration with us, playing at a standard way below his, but was always patient and understanding, encouraging and enthusiastic, with a wicked one-liner ready when needed.

In our one season in charge at Westport we finished a respectable fourth in the league and got to the Connacht Senior Cup Final. Unfortunately Frank couldn't be at Galway United's Terryland Park that day when we played Salthill Devon as he was being feted at Northampton Town.

Sadly we lost, I missed a sitter and I don't know whether Frank could have made a difference during the 90 minutes, but I do know he would have had a few sage words to help heal the wounds on the long, lonely bus journey home.

Frank never wanted to be involved with club management, and as well as Baltimore, he was seriously courted by other teams. He told me that he had little or no time for the back-slapping hypocrites that formed the boards of clubs and didn't feel at all comfortable in that environment. He had been exposed to their ways many times as a player and realised that their commitment to the bottom line was much more important than the person. Despite his best efforts on the pitch, he knew he was always 'up for sale', if the price was right.

'When they told me that they had received an offer and that I was to discuss terms, I knew that they didn't want me, so I decided that it were best for all if I left,' was his view. That explains my numerous schools and houses!

A couple of years later we were managing Ballina Town in the Connacht Senior League and having enjoyed a memorable victory over Westport United, which was special as Westport had sacked us in 1991 despite our comparative success that season, we travelled back to the Quay, in Westport, for a celebratory pint in Frank's local The Helm.

John the barman, a massive Westport United fan, served us glumly and as we were getting ready to leave I noticed a group of lads, with Yorkshire accents having a heated debate just behind me.

Eavesdropping, I overhear overheard that the debate was about football. Not football in general but specifically Halifax Town. 'He was the best player ever to play for Halifax,' claimed one of the gang, immediately challenged by his mate. 'Gi over, Frank bloody Large was the best, by a mile!' he boomed. As a statement it garnered general approval as several heads were nodded, and muffled 'Ayes' abounded as pints were sipped.

Flabbergasted, I broke into the debate, 'Excuse me, I say, but you see the fella over there at the bar?' Bemused nods and blank looks followed. 'Well that is Frank Large!' I nearly got knocked over in the rush as they surrounded Frank, ordering more drinks and reminiscing about the good old days at The Shay over 40 years earlier. It appeared that they were all from Halifax, in Westport on a fishing trip and leaving the next day.

I managed to get away some time later but Frank wasn't so lucky and much, much later Mum was called to pick him up, slightly worse for wear.

I caught John later that week and he told me that meeting Frank made the lads' trip, they couldn't believe it. As for Frank, he just made it to work the next morning!

Before the 1995 season the club were playing a friendly against our local League of Ireland team Sligo Rovers. The match was at home in Belleek, and was played during the annual Ballina Salmon Festival, on a cracking summer's evening on the banks of the River Moy.

Sligo's manager Lawrie Sanchez, the winner of the FA Cup for Wimbledon in 1988, had assured me that he would be playing his best side and we prepared accordingly.

Preceding the game, a number of youth five-a-side finals were being played, and the fact that the medals were to be presented by the former Liverpool and England captain Emlyn Hughes ensured that there was a large and encouraging crowd. Fifteen minutes before kick-off I was in full flight, giving the pre-match team talk, naming the starting XI and instructing on individual and collective duties – Frank was on his knees giving one of the lads a pre-match rub. There was a loud knock on the door and club chairman Sean McCarthy popped his head in and beckoned me outside. Sean never normally got in the way this close to kick-off, so I stepped out to be told that Emlyn wanted to play.

I shook my head and quickly assessed the situation, nodded at Sean and stepped back inside. I told the lads and asked hopefully if anybody wanted to let Emlyn take their place. There was silence as fingernails and boots were examined in minute detail. I did the only thing I could and pulled myself out of the starting line-up before re-organising the team.

Three minutes later Emlyn, by this point aged 47 but still looking in good shape, entered with a smile as ever on his face, was introduced and thanked me while shaking my hand. I told him he would be playing at left-back and threw him a shirt.

As he began to change he noticed Frank and scratched his head as he attempted to put a name to the face. Suddenly he blurted out, 'Bloody hell Frank what are you doing here?'

Frank began an explanation but was rudely interrupted by the shrill whistle of the referee, who wanted both teams out on the pitch. Emlyn had only just got his boots, socks and shorts on and as he walked out of the door he pulled our blue and white jersey over the top of his heavy cotton rugby top. It was late July and the temperature was in the high 70s.

As I took my unexpected seat in the dug-out, a solemn Sanchez barely nodded as he walked past. With Emlyn as our captain we won the toss and the first half began.

The first 12 minutes were fine as both sides tested each other out. Emlyn's touch and positioning looked solid enough, but the young Scottish right-winger started getting more of the ball and ran at him, exploiting his lack of pace. I can't say he was totally at fault for their first goal, but he certainly was for the second.

But, determined not to miss my chance to share the same pitch as 'Crazy Horse', I got into the action, just in time to see him signal to Frank to get him off.

We fought hard to get back into the match and I think we made a game of it, but my abiding memory is of Emlyn sitting next to Frank in the dug-out laughing and smiling as they caught up. Thirty years is a long time.

Unfortunately Emlyn couldn't manage to get out with us after the game but the Sligo players and management did. I thanked Lawrie for bringing them down and tried to strike up a conversation but failed miserably.

I concluded that he was just another miserable southerner, yet the truth was that he had just handed his resignation in to his chairman as he had accepted a coaching role at Wycombe Wanderers and had good reason to be so glum.

Frank only had another eight summers to go. He managed to make his debut in county cricket at the age of 59 when he helped set up Mayo County Cricket Club in 1999, winning the Leinster Minor Cup at Phoenix Park, Dublin, in the inaugural year. A natural who loved playing the game, bowling medium right-arm he topped the club's bowling averages with an amazing 7.8 and came second in the catching table.

And at last I had made it as a team-mate.

I was grateful for the time. The club still plays a regular match against a touring team from White City, the Frank Large Memorial Trophy, donated by Delphi Lodge.

I was lucky enough to share with him my two daughters and he watched them grow into beautiful young girls and enjoyed every minute of it. We met often and discussed life in general and football in particular.

I still miss his company and when I watch the occasional game on the TV, his incisive comments and shrewd observations, hunched over a pint, are cherished memories.

He was my dad and my hero.

Family friend Keiran Cooke finishes Frank's story:

'He lay on his bed – moved downstairs in the last weeks of his life – looking out the window at the view he loved. It was one of those special summer evenings when the west of Ireland flaunts its beauty to the world.

'The blue sky was turning purple in the fading light: a shaft of sun lit up a patch of bog. Far in the distance, the perfect conical shape of Croagh Patrick, Ireland's sacred mountain, was etched on the horizon.

'Frank was fading – and in pain. Somehow I knew this would be our last time together. What do you talk about at such moments? We discussed lawnmowers.

'We have a holiday home near Frank's house. In our absence, he'd looked after the rough patch of land, labouring away, determined to turn what is a piece of cow pasture into some sort of lawn.

'Frank never did anything by halves – or slowly. He'd more or less run behind his old four stroke mower as it bucked and heaved across the rough ground.

'Now I was trying to use the same mower: as he lay on his bed, he was anxious,even as his breath faded, to tell me how to start it – without having my arm ripped off – how to use the choke and how to use the bit of coat hanger he'd fitted to the engine which acted as a throttle. I moved to the door, wanting him to rest. Suddenly his voice boomed out, just as if he was calling for the ball, running full tilt towards the penalty area.

'"And you can keep the bugger," he said. Those words about a mower were the last I heard from Frank.

'Frank and I came from very different worlds. Me half Irish, half English (I've never been sure which side predominates), sent away to public schools (from which I gained little save a dislike of authority and discipline), eventually joining the BBC and then the *Financial Times*.

'Frank a Leeds man to the core, who had to struggle through life, getting his hands dirty and eventually, through his football skills, finding other worlds. Yet from the first time we met – over a drink in the grand lounge of the Irish fishing lodge where Frank acted as gardener and general factotum – there was a connection.

'We began by talking about Leicester City. My father, before his rise up the business ladder, had worked at one stage in his youth in what was once, pre-war Leicester's thriving hosiery industry. He'd maintained an emotional connection to the city. My father was not a big football fan and was often too busy with job or garden to give up a Saturday to go to a match. But on special occasions he'd be persuaded – and Leicester were the natural choice of team.

'Frank had yet to move to Leicester when I was watching the team in the early 1960s but he'd recall all the players. Strange sitting there in a valley in the west of Ireland more than 30 years later and finding the names coming back, like the words of a long ago song.

'Georgie Meek, a small darting winger who'd set the pitch alight with a lightning run up the touchline.

Frank McLintock, the solid centre-half. The legendary Gordon Banks in goal.

'"And who was that Stringfellow bloke?" I'd ask. Frank, taking another gulp of his whiskey, would give a quick summing up of the player's game. His talents, his weaknesses.

'Over the following years, we'd meet for a pint – or two – in the local town. Frank might have one eye on the match on TV.

'There was nothing long-winded about Frank. Nothing boastful.

'"Georgie Best? We'd be having a go at each other in the tunnel before the game, the boots scuffing the legs," Frank would say matter of factly. "It were all part of it."

'He could have been describing a village kick-about, not a First Division encounter in front of thousands. At times you had to coax the memories out of him.

'What did he feel about the way footballers are pampered – and paid – these days compared with the rough and tumble and minimal earnings of his playing days? Did he resent all the Ferraris, trophy women and bling?

'"Good luck to them," he said. "But I wouldn't want to be playing now. I had a great time – there were ups and downs but football were good to me."

'Frank had no bitterness whether it concerned football past and present or his sad diagnosis and months of treatment.

'Cancer doesn't just strike the frail and infirm and unfit. It targets everyone. Yet when news of Frank's illness came through it was a shock. Frank was one of the fittest 60-year-olds I'd ever met.

'I'd try embarrassed and awkward, to express concern about the state of play. Frank would have none of it.

'"Everything is going great," he'd say. "The tests are looking good." He'd overwhelm you with his positive approach to the disease that was eating away at him.

'And we'd quickly move on to other things – and to another pint. On TV a goalscoring chance had just been missed.

'"Look at him standing around dithering. Why doesn't he just leather it?"

'When he'd given up football and saved enough from his work in factories and in other jobs, Frank had his eye on Spain for a bit of mid-life rest and recreation. Aileen, his wife (of Irish parents) had other ideas.

'The weather in the west of Ireland is not exactly Costa Brava-like. But Frank threw himself into life in County Mayo with enthusiasm, as if he was running on to the pitch at a new club, wanting to make his mark, to enjoy every minute.

'He'd dash about the narrow roads, always on time or ahead of it – a very strange phenomenon in the west of Ireland. He'd treat everyone the same – Frank was incapable of acting a role, of being anyone but himself.

'One time, at the fishing lodge where he worked, Prince Charles came to stay. The visit was supposed to be top secret but few things go unnoticed in rural

Ireland. Frank, intent on his job, hadn't bothered to listen to the gossip.

'He was put to cleaning a boat His Royal Highness may use. Frank got fed up with all the painting and polishing.

'"Look," said Frank to the boss. "Fit for a bloody prince." Later Frank would laugh at his own naivete.

'I didn't have a sombre suit to wear for Frank's funeral – only a second hand, old tweed jacket which, by the look of its loud colours probably once belonged to a high-profile bookie. Standing there, singing away, I thought I could hear Frank laughing.

'And the mower? It's still going strong, all these years later. I run, push and heave behind it as it thrashes determinedly away. And think of Frank, an ordinary, extraordinary man.'